MEMORIES

AND FORGETFULNESS

BOOK ONE

LETTERS FROM TRAVIS

BOOK TWO

FAILING MEMORY

MEMORIES

AND FORGETFULNESS

Cover Picture:
Sarah, Travis and
Margaret (their Mother) Circa 1971

By Larry Calkins

MEMORIES AND FORGETFULNESS

ISBN: 978-1-7344718-1-6

Published by:

Larry Calkins

This book is dedicated to:

My wife and children

Acknowledgement

I would like to thank Yuvonne C. Brooks, Ed.D. for reviewing, editing and mentoring me through the writing of this book. She has provided me with insight and responsible guidance in the development of this material. I appreciate her encouragement and wisdom as well as hearing about her life experiences, writings, educational pursuits and teaching young minds. Most of all, I appreciate the fun we had talking, commiserating and laughing together as we worked diligently to address our mission.

MEMORIES AND FORGETFULNESS

MEMORIES AND FORGETFULNESS

CONTENTS

MEMORIES AND FORGETFULNESS

MEMORIES AND FORGETFULNESS

CONTENTS   PAGE

PROLOGUE

My father, Travis wrote letters most of his life. He penned many of them to my Aunt Sarah, his sister, around the time of my grandmother's (Margaret) dementia and passing. Dad continued to write letters when he was first diagnosed with dementia and throughout his illness. Eventually, he could no longer write letters to my Aunt Sarah but he left a wonderful legacy of his words which inspired this story.

Book One, Letters From Travis, provides some of those accounts. The correspondence chronicles both Dad and Aunt Sarah's coping with their mother's tragic illness. Also, he describes some of his day to day activities to Aunt Sarah by telling of his adventures. The writings display my father's personality, his worries, fears, joys and ambitions. Aunt Sarah and he continue with their letters after my grandmother's death in 1993. Then, Dad begins to explain his own forgetfulness to Aunt Sarah at the start of his dementia.

MEMORIES AND FORGETFULNESS

Each letter provides the reader with a glimpse into their lives, family and associates. My hope is that these letters will involve the reader in Aunt Sarah's and Dad's experiences.

When Dad understood he had the same disease as his mother, he told me, "Larry, use it or lose it." He said, "I kept writing to Sarah so I wouldn't lose my ability to write or to communicate." In 1997-98, he became a prolific writer. Aunt Sarah listened as well as responded in kind which strengthened their relationship.

***

MEMORIES AND FORGETFULNESS

Book Two, Failing Memory, tells my father's story after he was diagnosed with dementia. It includes my experiences with him and how I coped with his illness. Throughout the time, Dad was ill, I learned more about myself and what I might expect or even want from life. I describe my emotional involvement as Dad struggled with dementia and I with my grief.

When I fully comprehended the magnitude of my father's dementia, it hit me like "a ton of bricks." After accepting the fact that he had the disease, I was not sure how to help him cope through the illness. I made mistakes. However, I tried to remain positive, provide him the assurances he needed, create circumstances for his enjoyment and offer him compassion as we both traveled through the remainder of his life.

Sadie, my cousin and Aunt Sarah's daughter, recounted the time she visited my father in the nursing home. Dad had developed significant dementia. At the time, she asked me, "Does your father remember you when you visit with him." I told her, "It doesn't matter to me whether he did or did not." I continued, "What matters to me is that he is in a safe place, he has choices

3

about his surroundings and that he knows I love him. I am certain he knows I love him!"

Starting in 2009 and for an additional three years, Sadie told me that those comments stuck with her as she took care of her mother when she developed dementia like her mother's mother and mother's brother before her.

***

MEMORIES AND FORGETFULNESS

Unfortunately, Alzheimer's or dementia provides a difficult experience for the patient. For those of us who care and nourish relatives or friends, it offers little comfort. The disease is hard on everyone who observes the individuals who are afflicted. It is difficult to witness the deterioration of a person's mental and physical capabilities.

As Dad and I traveled on the road of dementia, I gained new respect for caregivers as I watched them attend to the needs of my grandmother and father. They woke patients, bathed, dressed, made meals, fed them and cleaned the rooms. Often, they had to lift patients in and out of wheelchairs or beds. These workers deserve our admiration and respect.

MEMORIES AND FORGETFULNESS

MEMORIES AND FORGETFULNESS

BOOK ONE
LETTERS FROM TRAVIS

1939 Travis *Circa 1988 Travis, Lucia* *1937 Sarah*
and Margaret (Travis' Mother)

MEMORIES AND FORGETFULNESS

LETTERS FROM TRAVIS

CHAPTER 1 – STEPPING BACK IN TIME

In a suburb of Boston, Massachusetts, the love between the two siblings, Travis and Sarah, eventually known as my father and Aunt Sarah, stemmed from a close family connection throughout their young lives. Giles, my grandfather, was a doting father and Margaret, my grandmother, a loving mother, until their divorce during The Depression.

One day, my great grandmother came to their home and stated that my grandfather had lost all his money during The Depression and my grandmother needed to divorce her husband. The abrupt dismissal of Travis and Sarah's father from the household threw the family into a new paradigm of dependency on my grandmother's, Margaret, parents.

That did not last long because my grandmother being independent with a sharp mind and strong fortitude ventured out on her own to tutor children at a friend's home on Cumberland Island in Georgia. The Cumberland Island experience lasted for nearly a year until my great grandfather, Margaret's father, turned ill. When they resumed life in New England, my father and Aunt Sarah attended school in Fairhaven, MA. They stayed there for a couple of years, until my father entered high school. My grandmother was employed as a matron at Moses Brown High School and my father became a student at the same school which was for all-boys at that time. Aunt Sarah entered Lincoln, the counterpart to Moses Brown for girls.

After graduating from Moses Brown High School, my father with a friend took off to Southern California where my grandfather lived and worked. He secured a job manufacturing airplanes and happily enjoyed the California sun. Aunt Sarah and my grandmother followed my father to Southern California to be with my grandfather where my grandmother remarried my grandfather. Aunt Sarah was able to work for one of the airlines because she had had recently graduated from high school.

My father wrote a brief history that describes his life after high school graduation. He was drafted into the Army Air Corps during WWII, attended Washington State College (WSC) and then married his life partner,

LETTERS FROM TRAVIS

Lucia, who was my mother.

History of Travis Calkins after High School

     I was drafted in 1943 at the age of 19 to serve in the U.S. Army in WWII. At that time, draftees were allowed to apply for pilot training. I took advantage of that opportunity. In due course, I graduated from flight school and was sent immediately to the European Theater of Operations (ETO) where I was assigned duty flying troops and cargo on a daily basis in C-47 transport aircrafts between 1944 and 1945.

     I was discharged from the Army in 1946 and became a student at Washington State College (WSC) on the GI Bill. I graduated with degrees in Psychology and Education in 1949 and 1950. When I first entered the U.S. Army, as part of the initial training we Air Corp cadets were sent to Washington State College to improve our intellectual powers. I was housed in the late Ferry Hall where we amused ourselves by bothering the local coeds in between rigorous exercises sponsored by the, then, U.S. Air Corps. I remember one pretty coed was a girl named Eva who worked at the library and attracted my attention. She was a great incentive to my reading habits. After the war was over and I returned to WSC as a GI student, I met another girl, fell in love and we were married. The eerie thing is that unbeknownst to me, Eva turned out to be the sister of my wife.

     I served most of my working life as a teacher and a school administrator in Seattle.

Travis

My father's relationship with his sister remained

close throughout the years. From childhood, through the later years in his life, he wrote letters when they were apart. One of the first letters he wrote began when he joined the Army Air Corps during World War II. In flight school, he became enamored with his upper classmates and wished he were taking off with them as they graduated. Later as he flew cargo planes during the war, he would say England was always foggy and he often needed to land planes by instruments only. He jovially, wrote Sarah, his sister about the events showing his humor, imagination and personality.

Jan. 5, 1943

Dear Sarah,

Sorry to hear you're under the weather—If it's anything like the weather around here you must be in a bad way. There hasn't been a clear day at this field since they built the place— Come to think of it, I can't figure out why they did build it. But—we fly anyway. Why it got so cold up there the other day that my instructor's words froze as they came though the gosports and I kept hearing them all the way down. Far-fetched wasn't it?

Say you should have been there the other night when the upper class had their graduating banquet. It really was a kick. I wasn't supposed to go, but after the dinner was over, I sneaked in and listened to the shit my roommates put on as a take-off on their officers. As a final gesture of their regard they presented the three tactical officers with a fur-lined bedpan saying that they hoped the three of them could get together on it. On the bottom was painted "the class of 44E looks up to you."

Ah yes, I wish I were going with the boys. I'm afraid this place won't be worth living in after they're gone.

Day before yesterday, I took a check flight and when I came down the instructor said – "well let's call that your twenty hour check," so I passed the first hurdle. Now, there are two more here at primary. I have about thirty hours now.

Have you guys found a place to live yet? From what I hear gas is going to be so hard to get they're thinking of cutting out "A" coupons entirely. You'd better move someplace near your work. Why don't you get a defense house? Gotta Go.

Love

Travis

After the war, my father continued in the military reserves and attended college on the GI Bill. He found himself at Washington State College studying psychology. He fell in love and married my mother, Lucia and earned degrees in education and Psychology. He and my mother began a family.

Meanwhile, Aunt Sarah started a family of her own. She married Will Palmer Senior, who planned to make a career in the Army. Aunt Sarah often traveled with Uncle Will to many parts of the world, making her peace with the military life as a dutiful wife.

Sarah wrote letters from Saigon, Hawaii and other exotic places that kept my father and her parents abreast of their travels and circumstances. Dad followed suit, by writing letters that described his family life and experiences he had as a teacher in the Seattle area.

Between 1950 and 1975, my parents raised a family of four children. Always the educator, my father taught school initially in the Clarkston and a short while later in the Seattle School Districts, and then became an administrator for the Seattle district. Early in his career, to cajole school children into learning, he told war stories, used humor or the Socratic Method in his educational processes. I do not think he wanted to glorify war to his own children. So, with the exception of the war stories, he used similar techniques on his children to provide us with his expectations. Also, he could be direct in his instruction to us. My mother, an educator too, had high expectations of us kids, but used a stern yet loving manner to provide similar expectations.

My grandmother, pleasantly distracted our lives. In my early youth, she lived and worked in Los Angeles, California and we resided in Lake Forest Park, north of Seattle, Washington. During my early childhood, she worked at Bullocks as a seller and later a buyer of ladies garments. Consequently, we did not see her often in those years. But when we were able to be with her, she treated us as if we were royalty.

Her first marriage with my grandfather turned out to be a happy affair until he passed away in 1960. When my grandfather died, both my father and Aunt Sarah rushed to Los Angeles to be with their mother. Dad flew to Los Angeles from Seattle and Aunt Sarah from Hawaii.

Much later after he passed, when shown a picture of my grandfather, Grandmother said, "He always treated me well," in a nostalgic sort of way. Since then she had lived mostly alone and became an independent accomplished woman.

A few years later when Grandmother retired, she purchased a farm in Silverton, Oregon. At the ripe old age of 13, I enjoyed visiting her there during the summer. She put my siblings and me to work as farm hands usually hoeing weeds in the strawberries or tending the cows. My grandmother graciously paid us for the work as if we were real farm hands. Most likely, she lost money on the deal because we were not very efficient. The strawberries she grew were sold to a large jam and jelly manufacturer.

Distinctly, I remember one hot day in August that year, helping my father and his cousin bale hay in the field. I drove an old beat up, pickup truck with a gear shift and clutch for the first time around the field. My father instructed me on how to use the clutch. He explained how to place the gear lever into first and then let out the clutch ever so slowly to move to the next bale without causing the truck to buck or kill the engine. I herded the pickup to each bale of hay through the rough field as the two men loaded hay on the back of the pickup. Despite my efforts, the truck "herked and jerked" along as I tried to make the trip smooth; more often than not failing at the smooth part. I don't know how any of the bales stayed on the truck, but neither my father nor his cousin ever told me I drove poorly nor did they ever usurp or take over the job from me. They just encouraged me to continue. I am sure they were able to chuckle or even laugh about the misadventure later. It must have taken my father back to the time on Cumberland Island in Georgia when he first learned how to drive old jalopies and provide rides to the Island patrons.

My grandmother displayed her welcoming personality and never failed to make her grandchildren feel any less than princes or princesses. Her regal state of mind gave her the air of a Queen Bee who cared for each of her subjects, particularly her offspring and children of her offspring. Practical and efficient, she kept to a strict routine. Yet, she offered a fun side of her personality, playfully teasing us or simply enjoying aspects of our youthful natures. She appeared to enjoy our visits as much as we enjoyed visiting her. I remember her with a permanent smile and a happy nature that she shared with everyone she met. With her impish style, she would take us aside and treat us with her wisdom of how to manage in an often inhospitable world.

I remember one time when I did not want to eat a

particular vegetable or a casserole on my dinner plate, she called me aside, put her hand on my shoulder and said, "Here's what you do. You rave about the meal and tell the host or hostess what a wonderful experience you are having. You see, they worked very hard to prepare the meal and you want to acknowledge that fact." As I started to object, she interrupted and continued, "Instead of eating very much of it, all you need to do is to take your fork and mess up the food on your plate gently or maybe playfully. Once dinner is over, you tell the master of ceremonies that you couldn't eat another bite, acting like or stating you are very full. Then, after the meal and socialization, you go downtown to buy a hamburger or something later." The lesson included acting graciously as well as helping the hostess save face when they probably knew they had created a disaster. Satisfying your needs a little later was a lesson in delayed gratification.

My grandmother felt strongly about saying things in a way that helped others feel good about themselves or at least keep their self-esteem. In voicing, this strongly, held etiquette, she explained how the world became a little more pleasant, when others maintained their dignity—a set of values I hold today.

My father, who always looked for entrepreneurial opportunities, purchased real estate and fixer upper properties to rent or resell; making a few dollars on the side. He never picked properties in the high rent district; instead he chose properties that remained a little cheaper than those in the immediate Seattle area. He explored, researched and eventually purchased most of the properties north of Seattle, between Lake Forest Park and Bellingham, Washington.

One day, he found a property in Rockport along the Sauk River. It was a quaint little house with fruit trees in the front yard. When my grandmother decided she had enough of the business aspects of farm life in Silverton, she moved to the Rockport property to carry on the country lifestyle. There her prized Borzoi show dogs, who won ribbons, could roam in a fenced backyard. For us kids, the property abutted the Sauk River and we enjoyed walking the sandbars or along the meandering river bank.

MEMORIES AND FORGETFULNESS

Rockport was a romantic place which gave my grandmother a second chance to be happy in marriage. There she met a widower named Sam Heath. She remained happily married until he passed away. Incidentally, when my wife, Carrie, and I married in 1974, we held our wedding at Grandmother's homestead.

My father and Aunt Sarah remained connected by sharing stories about their respective families and their adventures. But it was always a joy to reconnect in person. One letter sometime after 1978 expresses one of those reunions. While Dad liked golf, he did not take golf as seriously as Uncle Will.

Travis Letter to Will & Sarah Draft – Unknown date after 1978

Dear Will and Sarah;

You could have knocked me over with a feather after the telephone call on Tuesday evening. I checked out my "boot" which I packed away in a box after I got home to be stored until after the house renovation. Lo and behold—there it was $7 into toe of the right shoe and I never knew it. When Sarah asked me how the boot felt, I didn't have a clue. I'd send it back, but that game might go on and on. Well, I thank you but I owed it to you. Really, the $7 wasn't what felt bad; what felt bad was playing ante-over one green after another that afternoon. I think that 7 iron must be a trick club. Yes, I'm sure that's the answer. I'm still debating whether I'll ever play golf again.

LETTERS FROM TRAVIS

We're in the midst of redoing our bedroom area and putting in a bay window in the eating space. It takes a lot of thought, preparing and haggling to get things the way you want them. Then we've got to put up with a couple of weeks of camping, in a dust bowl inside our own house, while the work takes place. Then, we have to put on the finishing touches after those guys leave. And all the time, I'm wanting to go over to Roslyn to explore the mountains and swim in the lake.

Travis

As time passed, my father's and Aunt Sarah's children grew from young kids to adults. There were weddings, children being born and grandchildren arriving year after year for both families.

MEMORIES AND FORGETFULNESS

CHAPTER 2 – GRANDMOTHER'S DEMENTIA

Later in my young adult life, Grandmother moved closer to Mother and Dad's home in the 1980's. First, it was in a house trailer near my old school Lakeside Middle School, then her next move was closer to downtown Lake Forest Park near Lake Washington between Lake Forest Park and Lake City, Washington. Grandmother remained there as delightful as she had always been until the doctor diagnosed her with having vascular dementia.

Periodically, Grandmother forgot important things and her problem solving abilities waned. My father became a defacto-caregiver who helped her with many needs but at the same time limited her travel. The world she had known became smaller and she did not venture out much. Grandmother felt her situation worsen and welcomed my father's intervention.

At that time, Dad hid her cigarettes and when she could not find them, she forgot to smoke. It did not cure her from smoking, but she smoked far less. Also,

MEMORIES AND FORGETFULNESS

Grandmother liked to have a little nip, a glass of wine or hard liquor, in the late afternoons after dinner. Since suffering with dementia she began enjoying the nips earlier in the day.

About this time, my father discussed with Aunt Sarah the need to keep Grandmother from driving. They feared she would get lost or cause an accident and not be able to cope with the tragedy. Dad and Aunt Sarah talked on the phone, wrote letters, and remained in constant communication during this period.

One day, my father visited my grandmother near her birthday. She asked my father how old she was. He said, "Why you are turning 84 years old, of course." She responded in disbelief with, "My, that is old!"

Finally, two significant milestones occurred in my grandmother's life in the late spring of 1986.

First, Dad gave Grandmother's car to my sister, Alva. I do not know if he had discussed it with Grandmother or just assumed that she eventually would forget about the car altogether, but the upshot rang clear. He removed the car out of the driveway of her house and

Grandmother kept complaining that someone stole her car.

Second, Dad and Aunt Sarah concluded that they needed to provide more active caregiving for Grandmother. They found a moderate-sized assisted living unit near my father's home. Somehow, Dad and Aunt Sarah received my grandmother's blessing to move her to the facility where she would be provided with meals, a bed, and around the clock attention. Dad hoped that she would interact with other residents, develop good friendships, focus on socializing and find enjoyment at the new home.

The care facility worked out well until one night about 2 a.m. Dad received a call that Grandmother had left the facility and could not be found. Dad threw on some clothes, grabbed his keys and drove to the facility to find Grandmother. He found her walking outside the care facility in her nightgown, in the pouring rain, befuddled and looking for help. As tired, wet and confused as she was, when she saw my father, she returned to a happy and joyful state.

MEMORIES AND FORGETFULNESS

From that experience, Dad and Aunt Sarah decided that another smaller facility may be better for her. In early 1987, Dad found one in Bothell. This quaint facility provided more intimate care with a higher staff to patient ratio. Grandmother could be watched carefully. The smaller room was decorated with old memorabilia from her childhood and early adult life. It looked somewhat like a dorm room from college days.

One weekend, I drove to Bothell to visit her at her new home. In the middle of a nice conversation, she kept asking me the same questions about how my work was going. I kept repeating the same answer and a little while later, with all the earnestness in her voice she would ask me the same or a slight variant of the same question. She still complained about her stolen vehicle claiming she saw other people driving her car as if I would do something about it. Finally out of the blue, she remarked, "Larry, I just don't know if I can handle all those little boys when they come back to school from summer break this year." I probed her mind asking her what she meant. Ultimately, I figured out she thought she was back at Moses Brown, over four, maybe five decades earlier, waiting for the students to come back to campus.

Clearly, she remembered the earlier time when she identified herself as a school house mother, or matron, at Moses Brown, where my father attended high school. Moses Brown educated boys in a boarding school setting. These students relied upon my grandmother to provide parenting advice, meter out discipline when required and provide general care for them. Likely, due to her new cozy and deep-rooted surroundings at this Bothell facility, she transported herself back to 1938 in her mind. Yet, she still felt 85 years old, and was fearful of her abilities to handle a group of rowdy boys.

I had no idea how to reassure her that she would be alright, and she did not have to deal with those boys anymore. I just listened and hoped my grandmother would be fine with the fearful ordeal that was taking place in her thoughts. I have often thought about that experience with my grandmother and wish I could go back to help her regain her sense of time and comfort her like she had done for me at an earlier age. I talked to my father about the incident and he explained that is how the dementia worked. These types of fears often resurface from time to time.

Shortly, after my visit in the spring of 1987, Dad took her to Texas to be near my Aunt Sarah. She kept Grandmother at her home for a while. Eventually, they placed her in another care home in Texas. More telephone conversations occurred and letters were written back and forth between Dad and Aunt Sarah to communicate the delicacies of caring for my grandmother. She had been independent and now she was confined to a home under watchful eyes with my aunt visiting her as often as she was able.

This letter written in June 1987 describes selling the mobile home on behalf of Grandmother and other items of interest. My father enjoyed attending a "Marriage Encounter" where couples explored how to love themselves, family members and others more deeply. Dr. Brown is Grandmother's Lake Forest Park physician.

LETTERS FROM TRAVIS

June 29, 1987

Dear Sarah and Mother,

    I enclose a new Earnest Money Agreement with the latest offer which Sarah said she thought would be satisfactory. Sorry it is a little delayed. Lucia and I spent the weekend at the conference called "Marriage Encounter" which Sarah said she had heard of. This is a weekend set aside for couples who wish to make good marriages even better by learning techniques of communication which put the sparkle back in a marriage. We went there, worked hard all weekend, listening, writing and dialoguing and were delighted with the results. If nothing else, I've got some good essays to talk about with my children. Hopefully, they'll see a difference in us as well.

    Mother should sign these papers, both the earnest money and the contingency agreement and deposit the check. In the meantime, we'll keep advertising and if we get a better offer we'll go with that unless the Meed's meet it. As soon as we get the papers back we'll take them to a lawyer and start him drawing up a contract. The Meed's also have to talk with and be accepted by the Mobile Home Park owner. I don't think that's a problem.

    Hope all is going well down there. Let me know if you want Dr. Brown's recommendation on any tests.

Love to all,

T

The next partial letter does not have a date on it and may have been written around the time of the transfer of Grandmother from Washington to Texas. Dad

29

hopes to be reimbursed for the money he had spent on nursing home care. Evidently, Aunt Sarah became Grandmother's power of attorney.

Travis Incomplete Letter to Sarah – Unknown Date

...copayment on the nursing home care of $204.00, so perhaps you could write me a reimbursement for that amount from Mother's account. We will get it back, I believe from AARP anyway, but not from Medicare. I will get you the exact amount due the retirement home for the month of July, but I need to check with Lena (the nursing home administrator) on that.

We won't make a premature judgement on this nursing home facility (a very fancy looking one, I might add), but at this stage my analysis of its total effectiveness leaves me with certain vague concerns. More on this later.

We must keep in mind what the enclosed info sheet says. Every day here reduces the Medicare total responsibility by that many days.

We told Mother about Mini's death today. She reacted with normal concern, but undoubtedly will not remember it tomorrow.

Hope all is well.

Love,

Travis

The next letter is from Aunt Sarah to my father. In the early spring of 1988, my father flew with my grandmother to New England to see family and to generate a renewed interest in the place where she, Aunt Sarah and my father were raised. She discusses Grandmother's excitement about visiting Aunty Marta. Aunty Marta, her good friend and sister-in-law, saw sights around Boston as well as the rest of the New England Area. They enjoyed going to places that were part of their childhood and young adult memories.

Dad and Aunt Sarah decide against putting grandmother into a nursing home and decided that she could stay with Aunt Sarah and go to a day center instead.

The letter continues. My cousin Anna, Aunt Sarah's youngest child, has a kitten who entertains Grandmother. She still is concerned about her car, believing it has been stolen. She sees people driving a car like hers in Texas and thinks it is the one she had owned. Her reaction to what she sees is to call Dad.

MEMORIES AND FORGETFULNESS

May 10, 1988

Dearest Travis and Lucia:

This letter has been about three weeks in the making... I don't know how time gets away from me, but it does and we're always about three reels behind. Anyway, I wanted to thank you both for the tremendous effort and thought you put into this visit. It really was quality time and even if Mother doesn't remember it all she was certainly aware of it at the time and appreciated it, I know. The visit to Boston she won't forget. It was a good experience and gave her a real mental boost. And of course the excitement didn't cease when you left.

I wrote to the bank (Rainier) for a copy of the check, Mother was supposed to have mailed to the IRS last year. I didn't say we weren't sure she wrote it. I just said she needed a photo copy of the check written March 5, 1987 immediately for the IRS. I thought that would grab their attention.

May 23 – well, it did grab their attention and yesterday I got a notice back that they looked all the way from March 5th to September and found no cancelled check for $700 to the IRS. I guess that confirms our suspicion that she wrote it and didn't mail it. Anyway, I have the cancelled check for the $457.00 we wrote on the 15th of April and no notice of late payment so I guess we're OK.

Have you talked with your lawyer about putting her money into our names for future Medicare assistance? If we put her into the expensive nursing home at $57 per day it would be $1710 per month a little more than she has. The $50 home would be $1500 which she could handle. We're inching up on it. I have about $5000 more to put into a CD or Franklin Fund... an additional $35 a month. But, before that time comes (nursing home) I think the day care center will probably be the answer. She can handle that at $37 a day for 5 days a week and I can take care of her on weekends and of course she'd be home for dinner and we might be able to stretch that out and never have to use the nursing home. I just hate the idea of a nursing home.

Anyway, things are going along about the same. She is probably a little bit more confused as the weeks go by, some days she gets very irritated about the car and other days when she's calm she seems to understand that she forgets and she doesn't talk about the car...just about her cat and dog. We have Anna's kitty here which is taking her attention.

I'm sorry about the telephone calls. She will come in and get the telephone book, look up your number, come and tell me she can't find your number in the book, and I explain that it's in her address book. She then gets her address book, calls about 4 different numbers before she gets you. She gets very frustrated, but if I do it for her then I'm taking over and she's got to do things on her own. I have a feeling that the calls will be less frequent. I really don't think she'll be able to cope with even the phone. Although, she has days when she's sharper than others.

The other day I had to go shopping for panties and bras. She was in seventh heaven. First, because she could advise me and then because she could talk to the salesgirl about Bullocks: On-the-other-hand, I took her out to lunch with the "girls" Friday, to a very nice place on the strip...we spent about two hours over a very nice lunch... got home and that was the day she started calling you about the car! I don't know how to figure it!

Well, pretty soon Sadie will be here and that will be another bright spot. Incidentally, she's not bringing Mother up to Seattle in August. I just don't think I can coordinate that with a trip. We'll do something else. Either get a woman in to take care of her when and if we decide to go or arrange a couple of weeks in a nursing home...then we won't have to work it around someone else's schedule. Besides Sadie's time is fairly limited. She has to be back in Portland on the 3rd to meet her husband and son to look over colleges and then back home on the 5th to go to work. Her "summer" is awfully short by the time she takes the courses she has to complete to satisfy her job requirements and then gets back for registration in August.

Anna did well this semester with a 3.25 GPA. She's all set for her research work this summer with one of the professors...which will earn 6 credits. And then she's a full senior next year! She's really happy with herself...

Have a good time with your grandkids...this should be a fun summer for you two. Thanks for meeting my grandson at the plane I hear you are planning when he comes to Seattle. We're meeting him on the 30th of June on his way to Atlanta...and then of course will have him for the week in July when Sadie gets here.

Lots of love to you both,

Sarah

Further, the last part of Aunt Sarah's letter written in May 1988 discusses my other cousin, Sadie (my age). Sadie plans a trip to Texas to visit with her mother and grandmother in August. Aunt Sarah calls it a bright spot for Grandmother. Initially, Sadie and Aunt Sarah talked about bringing Grandmother to Seattle in August to visit Dad. I could imagine the three generations of ladies laughing and carrying on like school girls all the way from town to town and city to city as they made their way north from Texas. However, Aunt Sarah thought better of the idea, stating she could not coordinate the trip. My grandmother's dementia may have meant extra work caring for her, and making sure someone would attend to her needs. Frequent stops and breaks would be required throughout the grueling trip. Grandmother would certainly be anxious because she may not know where she was and what she was doing.

If they decided to go on the trip, Aunt Sarah figured she would have a woman to care for Grandmother or arrange for her to spend a couple of weeks in a nursing home.

Further, Aunt Sarah stated Sadie needed to be back in Portland on the 3rd so that she could meet her son and look over colleges. Then, it was back to Anchorage, Alaska on the 5th to return to work. As an educator, her "summer" is cut short by the time she takes the courses she must complete to satisfy her job requirements and then get back for registration in August.

MEMORIES AND FORGETFULNESS

LETTERS FROM TRAVIS

CHAPTER 3 – 1990 AGITATED

In 1990, Aunt Sarah decided to place Grandmother in a nursing facility near her home in Dallas, Texas. It was too much to provide care for her mother and keep up daily activities. It meant that Aunt Sarah visited Grandmother often and kept my father informed as to the progress or decline of their mother.

Dad held a sincere desire to help his sister from afar, but it was impossible for him to keep abreast of the day to day workings and so he relied on Aunt Sarah to provide direct supervision of their mother's situation. Although, periodically he traveled to Texas and offered suggestions to help, Sarah took most of the responsibility for Grandmother's wellbeing.

June 18, 1990

Dearest Sarah:

Nice to talk with you yesterday. I was naturally disappointed to learn that the nursing home is having so much of a problem dealing with Mother, but it's got to be faced and I want to help in any way I can. I called Senior Information

---

Services this morning and they suggested we contact their counterpart in Dallas. You may have already done so, but in case you haven't their number and address:

> Senior Information Services
> 2121 Main Street, Suite 500
> Dallas, 75201
> Tel: 741-5244

It would seem to me that they might be a nonmedical resource that could give information on other placements if necessary and to help with constructive ideas. I'll keep probing from this end.

We're having the grandchildren from Oregon here later on. I bought a sailboat which we hope will entertain them. We're also refurbishing the Roslyn house and Steve's condominium and those projects promise to keep us well-organized for quite a while. I'm enclosing a poem that was put to music by a guy from our church for Father's Day. It struck home to me and I'm sure a large number of the fathers in the audience. We're all so damn busy doing whatever it is we do all the time while the children are growing up; we never become the real fathers we want to be—always putting it off to a later date. Then, all of a sudden we find the kids are all grown up and we've missed the opportunity and now they don't have time for us What a tragedy—we're schmardt—too late.

Keep the faith and have a good summer. I'll keep in touch.

Love,

Travis

The next two letters surprised me. Grandmother became agitated and difficult to handle at this stage of her life in the care facility. My father discusses with Aunt Sarah how my grandmother was mistreated as a child. Evidently, Aunt Sarah sent a letter detailing a doctor's visit (presumably a psychiatrist) who delved into my grandmother's mind and provided insights into her childhood and the treatment she received as a youngster. It makes some sense, but a journal that my great grandmother wrote about my grandmother's formative years does not hint at any abuse or disgust with her. The journal made it sound like a mild and joyous upbringing.

Still, there must have been something to it because a "doctor" has discovered deep anger in my grandmother. The anger was suppressed around her grandchildren, because I never had an experience where she displayed anger around me. I always thought of her as being worldly, kind, and without a hint of malice against herself or directed toward other people.

July 27, 1990

Dearest Sarah:

For all the fact that our medical system is a disgrace and a rip-off, Mother does seem to have been helped at the hospital and your letter sounded optimistic (my medical plan, is an

---

exception—quite reasonable because I've been in it for 35 years.)

I was interested in the doctor's analysis about Mother's mistreatment as a child. It may have been more complicated than that. You and I know that Grandmother (my great grandmother) had a preference for boys and treated Mother as "dumb"—even when she was an adult. Grandfather, on the other hand, spoiled Mother and probably wasn't to' harsh on her, although I've always suspected that he may have had genetic problems; he was a terror to most people. The moral rigidity of New Englanders of that time was fierce and had too much guilt all the way around. Nobody, including the doctor, knows the complete story. But, at all events, I agree; the anger goes way back.

Well, if you keep busy you don't have time to notice the gray hair. A friend asked me how old I was, and when I told him, he said, "beautiful! You walk up hills like a young man." I immediately handed him a $5 bill.

We're sending a package to you for Mother. I never know what to send and couldn't find some of the things you suggested. Mother characterized previous packages as "junk". They apparently made an impression that stayed with her. If these things aren't useful throw them away. Save the picture of of our Great Grandmother (your namesake), however. You'll want that when Mother is through with it.

I was glad to hear about Sadie's trip to Europe. But to me the interesting part (of Europe) would be the newly released Eastern Bloc countries. The fabulous changes that have occurred have been mind-boggling! We've seen half a century of historical change compressed into a few months. I'd give my little toe to have been there and watched it in person (from a safe distance, of course).

When I see the terrible yearning for what I've got and my modest life style in a good man's eyes, it makes me restless and I want to know the situation first hand.

Enough of that! Write me again. I love your letters.

Love to all,

T.

Dad continues to go back over the psychiatric hospital stay of Grandmother where he learned about her childhood trauma. Both he and Aunt Sarah wrestle with how best to handle their mother's trauma and how best to care for her.

Also, he shares memories about "borrowing" a couple of exchange students from Japan, took them to the Space Needle, having them over for dinner and being serenaded by them as they played the piano.

August 10, 1990

Dearest Sarah:

Thank you for the extensive summary of the "Mother in the Psychiatric Hospital" saga. It is a long, mysterious and primarily futile story with a sad ending i.e. a not very hopeful peek at the future—certainly no self-evident solutions. But, I am glad you worked with Mother's doctor. He seems to at least have some realistic notion of what may be happening. You're probably right. If we had hired a male attendant when she was living by the river, she might still be there and relatively happy. Well, it just goes to show how life is nothing but a crapshoot for us all…and if you're lucky you make the right choices, but your chances are only 50% if that.

Not content with having regular guests, the next weekend we went to the house of a friend of mine who had two teenage girl's from Japan staying with him as exchange students. So Lucia and I borrowed the students for an afternoon and took them to see the Space Needle and the Seattle Center. They came to our place for supper and played a piano concert for us, both being talented musicians. So, this means we'll have to go to Japan to see our Japanese friends as well as other worldly places. This international hanky-panky may be running into money before we're through—what with the increase in costs of energy and all.

Like Mother, I was born to be rich and spend a lot of money. Unlike Mother, I know the value of a buck and how to keep some of it for my old age. However, I think Uncle Sam knows how to pry open my tight fist anyway, so perhaps Mother has the right idea after all. You might as well throw it around, they're not going to let you keep it anyway. Thanks again, for the informative letter. Have a good summer.

Love to everybody there.

Travis and Lucia

Dad and Aunt Sarah continued to struggle with

Grandmother's situation in Texas. Caregivers and nursing home staff became befuddled with how to best care for Grandmother. Although, I remember her *warmly* and as a charming and delightful woman, I can see how she would struggle with caregivers. As an independent woman who made decisions for herself without relying on others it was probably upsetting, frustrating and irritating for her. Now, she is fully dependent on other individuals at this late stage in life. Aunt Sarah busily smoothed the ruffled feathers of the caregivers and helped with Grandmother's basic needs.

As an aside, Dad describes his experiences with being on a jury. He is impressed with the seriousness of the jurors.

November 4, 1990

Dearest Sarah:

Thanks for the detailed letter on Mother's situation. I can see that it keeps you busy just being a backup to the nursing home personnel. What happens in those cases where the family rarely shows up? Well, in Mother's case your efforts are much appreciated from this end. When I read the letter to Alva, big tears welled up in her eyes. I read these things to some of the family so they get a visual picture of a reality they may not know much about. It's good training for them.

MEMORIES AND FORGETFULNESS

I've been on jury duty for two weeks for which I was paid all of $80. I'm not sure why Lucia got $134 for her two weeks, except I think old men get discriminated against these days. I'm going to write a letter to my congressman about this right after I vote him out of office for being an incumbent.

There was a very nice looking gal on one of the panels who was a dead ringer for you in both looks and actions. I promptly nominated her for foreman and she did a good job.

I was quite impressed with how seriously most of the jurors took their work and how carefully they tried to evaluate the cases—particularly how the law applied to the case in point. The lawyers' histrionics didn't appear to me to sway many people, and the judge's directions were taken very seriously.

Glad to hear you're all doing fine.

Love to you all!

Travis

As 1990 comes to a close, Aunt Sarah summarizes the year by describing their travels and highlights. We can only imagine the intervening months and the struggles she has had; assuring care for Grandmother. Aunt Sarah and my father have learned more about their mother than they probably wanted to know, yet still it rounds out their knowledge of who she was before they were born and who she has become. Dad appreciates his sister's caring nature, realizing he could not have been the hands on manager of his mother's care that his sister has provided. He hopes that his support, both verbally and in writing will help to sustain her; knowing how hard it is to be the responsible party.

<u>Sarah's Christmas Card to Dad</u>

Christmas 1990

Dearest Family,

This has been a truly busy year—with events we could never have foreseen. From my trip to Seattle to your trip to Dallas, to Mother's trip to the nursing home and another trip to a psychiatric hospital—and finally in Nov. Will's trip to California to help out with his sister, when she returned home after back surgery! Intersperse those trips with trips to McKinney to babysit and trips to the nursing home to do Mother—and your trips to Pendleton, SD, Colorado and, of course, the retirement home and we've put in a few miles! And come December 31st, I will make my last trip to the Club as an employee—I have given my official notice and filed for Social Security Retirement which I should be receiving any day now—and I will be a member of that ever increasing group of SS Beneficiaries—Rah, Rah, Rah!

I decorated Mother's room with a beautiful wreath and a poinsettia plant. I'm not sure she really notices it, but I do—and so do the staff—and since they know I care, perhaps they will care a bit more! And when I say she may not notice—sometimes she doesn't even notice when I'm there, and wheels herself out of the room, in her own imaginary world, as unaware of me as she is the pictures on the wall. And then, there are other times when she will take Daddy's picture when

MEMORIES AND FORGETFULNESS

I hand it to her and with eyes brimming say "I miss him; he was so good to me"—Anyway, she would certainly send her love and warmest Christmas wishes if she could. Anna and I were there on Thanksgiving. I took pumpkin chiffon pie to her and the staff. She doesn't really recognize Anna now—and, sometimes she knows I'm Sarah and sometimes she just knows I'm someone in the family—maybe "Mother". But she's not agitated anymore, and that's a much happier condition—She's on another less potent medication Mellaril—which seems to be working fine.

Best Love to you and all from all of us.

Sarah and Will

LETTERS FROM TRAVIS

CHAPTER 4 – 1991 MENTAL DECLINE

The following year, my father and mother planned a trip to see Aunt Sarah and Grandmother. The letter states that she seems to be doing much better. Her condition has stabilized without showing symptoms of being anxious and is more comfortable with her situation in the nursing home. Aunt Sarah pays attention to the little things like ice cream and fresh fruit in Grandmother's diet.

April 15, 1991

Dearest Lucia and Travis,

We got your letter—and will be at the airport on May 8, at 7:19—Delta Flt 1158! It should be a perfect time weather wise her in Dallas—we're warm but not devastatingly hot til June.

Well, we're looking forward to your visit—I read your letter to mother and she was quite pleased—and I tell her again each time I see her—and it's always news to her. She's eating much better now. Yesterday I took ice cream over to her. They don't get ice cream or fresh fruit—one of my biggest complaints—and Mother loves ice cream.

MEMORIES AND FORGETFULNESS

> Well, must get cracking here—the peach tree needs spraying—the birds need food—and I need to get dressed!
>
> Love,
>
> Sarah

Aunt Sarah follows with another letter that updates Dad on life at the nursing home and Grandmother's progress. Apparently, the Director of the nursing home called a meeting of family members of the residents to inform them about the progress and changes at the facility.

Grandmother has become more forgetful, unable to remember the pictures of her grandchildren and has lost most of her problem solving skills. Mentally, she has "stepped down" from being the vibrant woman she was at one time and readily accepts help from caregivers.

> May 26, 1991
>
> Dearest Lucia and Travis,
>
> Seems like yesterday that you were here—but it was two weeks ago!—and what a whirlwind visit. We crammed about as much as we could into five days. They didn't call me "the tour director" in Spain for nothing!

I was glad you got to see the nursing home "in action"—and that you agree with me that it's about as good a place for mother, all things considered, as any. She's not locked up in an Alzheimer's wing—in fact now they have taken the restraining vest off her and she seems to know that she needs the wheelchair for support but can get out if it to go to the bathroom! (As she did when I was there yesterday, all by herself, unaided!) I showed her the pictures and she recognized both of you. I took her outside, it was a beautiful day—I mentioned Bill, Sadie and Anna and she couldn't remember them at all—So it goes.

The meeting that Rodney Harris called on the 16th was attended by about a dozen people—out of the 72 people we called—and only 3 council members—That is discouraging! And the head nurse, Lee Frazier, the heavy set one (white) is resigning—I hope she is replaced with a more active one.

And thank you, both, again for making the trip down here—It was quite a stunt in your busy lives.

Love to you both,

Sarah

As Grandmother becomes more compliant and accepting of the nursing facility, Dad and Aunt Sarah relax a little. Still, Aunt Sarah remains active in the nursing home activities and offers suggestions on how to improve the facility. She takes an active interest in the care Grandmother receives and tries to suggest improvements that are not only good for her mother, but also for the rest of the residents.

Dad writes to his mother, but requires his sister's ability to interpret, by explaining the activities of family members and other fine points in the letter. He writes about the mother and daughter banquet where he wasn't invited. But, he explains his computer and the chess game he plays with my brother. He stated he visited his old alma mater during the winter.

While family activities are paramount in Dad and Mom's life, Dad knows his mother would be interested and maybe even remember Mr. Thomas the Headmaster at Moses Brown since she had been a matron at the school for many years. Her memory and problem solving skills are not as sharp as they once were, so Dad peppered the letter with names of other retired teachers. He hoped that she would possibly remember them and this might eke out any memory in her brain.

He explains he will be attending a graduation of his oldest granddaughter. Explaining that he knows each of his children have warm and fond memories of his mother, he hopes that she will find some joy or glimmer of her old self, spiced with happy times she may remember.

May 29, 1991

Dearest Mother:

I'm sending this to Sarah to bring over to your place, so that she can go over it and fill in anything I leave out.

Lucia is over at the church tonight with Alva. They are having a mother-daughter banquet there, so naturally I wasn't invited. Steve is here with me. He's a computer buff and is dickering around with the computer. Among other things the computer will display a chess board with all the chessmen pictured in their places. By pressing certain keys like on a typewriter, you can make the chess pieces move where you want them to go, thus playing a chess game either against another person or against the chess computer itself. Strangely enough the computer can figure out how to contest you move, and if you're not careful, beat you at the game. I can beat Steve, but so far haven't been able to beat the computer.

I'm not sure whether I wrote you that I visited Moses Brown this winter on my 50th graduation reunion. Mr. Thomas was still around the school not of course as headmaster, but as a sort of elder statesman. He remembered my name and asked how you were. Mr. Howe and Ted Whitford also were still around the school also as retired teachers. In fact, Mr. Howe's daughter lives in Seattle and I have talked with her by phone since I got back.

Lucia's brothers and sisters are coming here next month for a family reunion, which we have every two years. They live in various states in the west—Oregon, California, Arizona and

---

Washington. They'll probably stay a couple of days and we'll take a ferry ride and perhaps play some golf. Mostly we'll sit around and tell what's happened in the last two years. Now they all have children and grandchildren, some of whom will also be here, so we keep up to date on the younger generation too.

Our oldest grandchild, Hettie is graduating from high school next week. We'll go to Oregon to see her get her diploma and to see mom and dad. We might go down by train, which is sort of fun and the station isn't far from their house. It's about an 8 hour trip.

We think about you often and hope things are going well with you. Sarah and Will are quite busy right now with the storage business they've acquired, but when things ease off a bit for them, we will come down to see you.

The children send their love. I wish they could all come to Texas to see you. They, however are struggling to raise their young families and it's difficult for them to get away. They all *think warm and fond thoughts* of "Grandma", however.

Love from us, too,

Travis and Lucia

The next letter provides insight into his mother's stature as a socialite with caregivers accommodating her every need at the nursing facility. He compliments Aunt Sarah on her leadership at the home as well. He then reiterates a quip about Mr. Thomas the headmaster at

LETTERS FROM TRAVIS

Moses Brown. It is one that he hopes his mother will enjoy.

September 7, 1991

Dearest Sarah and Mother:

Thank you for your newsy letter and the news publication you have now instituted. I'm really proud of you for doing such an outstanding job of organizing that place. Between your hard work and leadership and Mother's stature as Queen Bee, you're going to put that place on the map. When I'm ready for the treatment, it'll all be set up—I can hardly wait!

Alva is very excited to be coming to see you both on her way back from Disney World. Did I tell you how wonderfully she's raising our grandchildren? O.K. I'll shut up, but it'll be hard. But, we do think it's great that the cousins can compare notes on their respective houses, children, husbands, etc. etc. And Alva will love seeing you and Bill on her own. She also very much wants to see Mother.

I'll be working the polls later on this month and headed back east to Providence to the reunion in October. Tell Mother that Mr. Thomas is now 101 and sharp as a tack. He says the only trouble with being 101 is that everyone treats you like a baby and he says he's no baby.

Love to you both,

Travis

MEMORIES AND FORGETFULNESS

LETTERS FROM TRAVIS

CHAPTER 5 – 1992-1993 PASSINGS

When my father retired, he became interested in genealogy. At this time, he was "following in his father's footsteps" and other relatives on his mother's side to prepare a history about his ancestors. He looked through his father's papers and saw that they contained information that dated back to the landing of the Mayflower and beyond, tracing the family back to the kings and queens of England. As he compiled his version of both histories he wanted to see how his own childhood fit into the family's larger genealogical picture.

On October 31, 1992 my father wrote about his childhood and told stories with *fond memories* he shared with his sister over the years.

In 1929, before the big crash, Dad rented a small cottage on the north side of Cape Cod. I think it was near the town of East Dennis. The cottage was part of a large piece of shore-land called the Swett's estate. It included a stretch of beautiful curving beach with shallow water extending out in front of the house for a long way, especially at low tide. The large, white Swett's house was off to the East on a knoll a good distance from the cottage, but visible to it. That summer, the Cape was hit by a heavy Nor'easter. During the storm hundreds of lobsters were swept in close to shore. We kids would walk out in waist-high water, being careful where we stepped, see them at close range. I remember Dad carefully picking several of them up. We had a delicious dinner and lobster has been a favorite in our family ever since.

That summer the Swetts sold their place and held a big furniture auction which Dad helped to organize. He also bought from the estate several nice antiques, among them a pair of "spool" beds which Dad scraped down to the bare pine. They adorned our spare bedroom for years. Many years later I found an identical spool bed at an auction in Seattle. Of course, I couldn't resist it, and it now stands partially scraped, in one of the Roslyn house bedrooms.

In 1929 our family home was located in Waban, Mass, a subdivision of Newton, which is a suburb of Boston. Sarah and I were both, I think, born in the Newton hospital. I started school in Waban attending kindergarten, and first grade there. I remember walking to school even as a kindergarten kid. Much to my surprise upon return to the scene some 60 years later, I found that the distance from our house to the school was a good long way…at least a half mile. Schools provide busses for trips like that nowadays.

To me, the house looks just as it always did—a friendly Dutch colonial with its half-acre lot undoubtedly still hiding Mother's diamond engagement ring where presumably, I threw it from an upstairs window a long, long time ago. Nobody knows for sure, but I was always assumed to be the culprit\, and have lived with this presumed guilt all these years. For some reason the maid, or a serviceman or a guest were never mentioned as possible suspects. Sarah may even have swallowed it, and may be worth much more than she knows, but I never heard that theory advanced. I hope someone found it and is the richer for the finding. It would be a shame if it went down the toilet.

Sarah:

If this gets to maudlin or unconnected or just plain insipid, by all means, change it, reword it or eliminate whatever you would like. I only send it because I get an idea and take off.

Anyway, I think its fine.

Love,

T

In 1993, prior to the passing of their mother, Dad writes a letter to Aunt Sarah realizing his age and stature as the patriarch of his family. He describes his children to Aunt Sarah and their eventful lives. He begins with Alva's family.

March 8, 1993

Dearest Sarah:

Alva had her 34th birthday yesterday. The whole in-law tribe was there and at least a good part of the o clan, plus assorted friends and foes. My gosh, I can't believe my youngest is now 34. Why only yesterday I was changing her diapers— well, every once in a while. Her husband bought her a new car—well, almost new. The greenback I gave her was brand new—small, but NEW. The difference was that he couldn't afford the car, and I could afford five dollars. We had a great time. Alva's in-laws are a friendly bunch and the father-in-law and I get along well—he tells me corny jokes—and I laugh a lot. Incidentally, Mother's car is on its last legs. I guess it's all the hard use the boys gave it when they used to joyride past your house when Mother lived with you. Remember how she would see them driving past just about every day and call me up long distance to scream at me about it? I was always surprised how they could get back from Texas so quickly.

We have a female houseguest now. It's Steve's friend. She's staying in the downstairs bedroom and Lucia is very patient with her, but I have a feeling that she'll get sick of staying with a couple of old fogies very long. Steve very patiently drives her all over the place, becoming her private chauffer I am unused to that honor and am not quite as enthusiastic about the tremendous possibilities for public service this little task brings.

We hope things are now going well with Bill, Sadie and Anna. They are such nifty young people. We're very fond of them and wish we could see them more. How did we ever get out families spread out all over the place? It had something to do with the war and the depression, both of which should have happened to someone else. Now, if Dad hadn't gone to California..... No that won't work out right. If Dad hadn't gone to California, I'd have never gone into the Air Corps and that would have screwed up everything.

This nutty letter is really just to let you know that we're still around and love you. Hope all is going well and that things are back to normal down in Tyler. Keep the faith and don't play the ponies.

Love,

T

Sadly, shortly after the previous letter was written, Grandmother passed away on March 19, 1993. Dad flew to Texas to be with her on her last days. She passed with little fanfare in the arms of her daughter and son.

Dad writes in remembrance of his mother, "Margaret Heath was a singular and very special person. Her gracious and witty mannerisms, accented by a persuasive charm attracting attention wherever she went. People easily recognized her self-confidence, and poised demeanor, and seldom failed to want to know her better. Her seven grandchildren adored her, as did nearly all who knew her well."

My father and Aunt held a funeral for grandmother without much fanfare in Texas. Only a few people attended. After she passed, I gathered my siblings, invited my cousins and held a memorial in Lake Forest Park for our grandmother. Bill flew in to represent the Palmers. We included my Aunt Sarah by phone in the memorial.

MEMORIES AND FORGETFULNESS

After the funeral, Aunt Sarah wrote a letter to Dad.

Aunt Sarah's Letter to Dad after Grandmother's funeral

Sarah Palmer
Sat. AM 4/3/1993

Dearest Travis--

A quick note to let you know what's going on. On the way home from the airport, I stopped by the nursing home to ask for names of aids most closely associated with Mother on Halls 2 and 3. One of the aids gave me the attached list and suggested that I include a suggestion that they do not mention this gift to others so as to avoid hurt feelings—and to mail it to their homes— I didn't get the addresses until Wednesday the 31st because I was busy in McKinney, Tyler and the secretary at Nursing Home was on Jury Duty—So I went back and FINALLY got the addresses—I had already written the $20 checks and notes so got them mailed out that AM!

I have just done Mother's 92 Taxes—She owed $114— I couldn't believe that the Tax on her adjusted gross income of $751 was that much. Her gross was about $7000 and, of course, that doesn't include her non-taxable $7500 Social Security. I thought she might be eligible for "Credit for the Elderly", but if her Social Security was more than $5000 she wasn't eligible! Anyway, that's done.

I'm calling all of the doctors and labs and other hospital services that had anything to do with her latest hospital stay to make sure they file with AARP—so I can clean up her medical. I sent AARP deceased notice—also NY Life (Bullocks). I wrote all those who sent flowers, and some of our relatives. I'm going to write to Forest Lawn, the cemetery, to get started on the head stone. Anna can ascertain that it was done properly— when she gets out there. I want to get all the bills paid before I do the probate thing and I'll call our lawyer regarding that.

Now, the most gratifying thing has happened. Forgive me if I get wordy or repetitive—but I think we are making progress, and the "family" is still alive! Bill called his father last Wednesday. It was a very courageous thing for him to do and very possibly grandmother's death made him see how fragile we are and how think our blood ties are. Or perhaps it was his wise little sister's conversation with him shortly after her death—maybe our prayers—but he called—and they talked.

I was on my way to the nursing home so didn't hear all of the conversation, but the tone of Will's voice was moderate—non-confrontational and perhaps most important, honest. He (young) Bill then called me that night—and although he is still grasping around in a deep, dark hole, he's seeking the light and trying to put the past behind him.

I had a different theme for him to chew on—as I listened to his dredging up the gloomy past and the painful present. I suggested that if ever Grandmother left a legacy, it was one of joy. She never looked on the dark side of anything. She ventured into the unknown countless times—the Depression of the 1930's—her sojourn to Cumberland Island—tackling the job at Moses Brown. Then with pioneer spirit of her forefathers, left the security of New England for the great unknown of the west—embarked on a new career—another career in Oregon—another unknown in Rockport all with zest—undaunted courage—No Gloom in her life. What a legacy! What a lesson! And Bill listened. I also told him that there is one thing about Mothers: They never give up on their children. I can't speak for fathers, brothers, sisters, aunts or uncles, but I know about mothers. And I said that I look beyond the things he is saying today to six months from now, perhaps a year when he'll be thinking and feeling positive thoughts about himself and those around him—and I told him that I was confident that he would climb out of this abyss, and that it would be a sign of real growth and maturity, and then I said he needed a good belly laugh, that crying may release a lot of heartache—but that laughing was good for the soul.

I wasn't trying to be trite—but I think he has to lift himself up onto another plane—one of hope—not despair—and all of these things he just do himself. Others can't do it for him, but we're all supporting hi and we all love him. Anyway, we crawl before we walk—and he's crawling.

Want to get this in the mail before 2:30—or it won't go out til Monday—like all my letters last week!

All's well otherwise. I'll keep you posted on all developments. Thank you, again for coming down to Dallas. I have a lot of thoughts about those final hours—among which are that it is important to be there to help with that journey and to understand that it is not an end, but a continuation of a spirit and it brings that spirit so much closer.

Love to you all.

Sarah

I was impressed by Aunt Sarah and her discussion with her son, my cousin. He faced his fears with his father and then his mother described how grandmother's legacy was one of joy. How she forged a new life during the depression with two children without the help of a husband by her side. How she went to Cumberland Island in Georgia with her family, met the challenge of a single parent. Then, went back to New England to be a matron at Moses Brown providing a good education for her children. After her children graduated high school, she moved on to California, remarried became a sales person and a purchaser for a major department store. Then, undaunted she moved to Oregon to farm berries and then on to Rockport to retire and remarry. Aunt Sarah observed that there was no gloom in grandmother's life, simply perseverance. She left a legacy of joy and happiness for her family to see and share. My cousin listened and it began to change his life.

Sadly, Uncle Will, Aunt Sarah's husband, died later that fall. She has just finished or is in the process of finishing my grandmother's probate and now had to deal with the probate of her husband. The grief she must have felt after both their deaths in 1993 must have felt overwhelming at times. Aunt Sarah was strong like her mother. She displayed compassion toward her children and family members at this time when everyone was grieving. Her resiliency was unparalleled.

MEMORIES AND FORGETFULNESS

LETTERS FROM TRAVIS

CHAPTER 6 – 1994-1996 FAMILY

In January, Dad writes to his sister. At the end of the letter, he describes her family's closeness after Uncle Will's death. Further, he compliments her son, my cousin, about the fact that he has a sense of proportion as well as excellent analytical skills about people and situations. Dad is very impressed with his nephew.

Jan. 15, 1994

Dearest Sarah:

Before we forget it, we want to thank you for the National Geographic gift. It makes a great gift because there are hours of fascinating adventure in its pages... and you keep reading it over the years—it never gets old. We appreciate your thoughtfulness.

We're also in the middle of tax time. For the past 50 years, I've done my own taxes. This year I decided to let someone else do them for me. The problem is the guy's finding all kinds of things he needs to change in order (he says) to gain advantages I'd overlooked. And it's turning into a bigger job than I thought. Well, we'll see. If he charges me a lot but makes more gain than he charges, I guess I can't complain.

You are absolutely right about your son, Bill. He impressed all of us mightily in San Diego and here, as well, with his sense of proportion, his analytical skills about people, and his ability to find out what was needed—and do it. To boot he's a good guy and fits in like and old shoe. I'm so glad you all had that time of closeness and support for one another after the funeral. It will sustain you all mightily—and things will look up from now on—I predict.

Love,

T

Again, in February, Dad writes Aunt Sarah discusses the living trust concept with her and reiterates the closeness of her family. Aunt Sarah and her three children came together and developed a time of renewal. He explains that he and my mother are very fond of all three of her children.

Feb 9, 1994

Dearest Sarah:

How nice you called last night. I'm glad you liked the little book of homilies... I thought you might. You're really a very literary person, who, like myself, is intrigued with a meaningful phrase that can inspire and give a person a speck of light to guide him through the darkness.

You mentioned that you were somewhat disenchanted with the "living trust" idea which you had just completed before Will died. Thinking of all the work you did when Mother died without a trust, I thought you might have felt that it was awfully nice not to have to go through that again with

Will's passing. Could you comment on that in a few words – yes or no? I'd like to know whether I'm getting a snow job from the "living trust" people.

We nearly went ahead with a trust about three years ago, but held off because we couldn't figure out how much the salesmen were telling us was fact and how much was bull.

As I think I mentioned before, we felt that your kids really came together as a close-knit clan after Will's death and that a time of renewal was at hand. I surely hope that is true. We're very fond of then, all three, and wish them and you great renewal and peace I the coming years. You all deserve that, and Lucia and I will be praying that the peace of God's love will descend upon you all.

Warm wishes,

T

In January 1996, since Dad had not written his sister for quite a while, my mother decides it is time to keep the correspondence going. In particular, she wanted to thank Aunt Sarah for the recent gifts they had received at Christmas time.

Mother's Note to Sarah – Jan 5, 1996

Dear Sarah;

There is magic in the air here after Travis has had a visit on the telephone with you. He's enjoying a 600 piece puzzle; twice a week moving that big vacuum cleaner about, cleaning out church.

Yesterday he had a day alone to do as he wanted—mail letters get headlight replaced in truck etc. Guess the mechanic needs to give him a hand on the truck light.

So far it's a mild winter here and only light rain, so driving is simplified. It is a warmer Seattle than usual.

Your gift arrived—a nice basket tray full of fruits, something needed in our menu. I especially like the black figs and dates all arranged on the platter without pulling out of a box. It is so inviting sitting there on the counter by the refrigerator. Thank you for your gift. Also, we are pleased you sent pictures of our little boys—portrait of our sons and others.

Picture placed in some order is on my agenda, after piano lessons to the children and various other PTA etc. "jobs". A reward for judging reflections theme was a gift certificate to Starbucks. I'll take my friend Marge out for a treat.

Our best for your New Year!

With Love

Lucia and Travis

In February Dad writes Aunt Sarah after he and my mother returned from visiting us in Bend Oregon.

They enjoyed spending time with me and my youngest daughter, Emma. Carrie was away on a trip and the older two children were in college.

Feb. 27, 1996

Dearest Sarah:

It seems that we're all taking to the highways to visit our children these days. Lucia and I just returned from Bend, Oregon, where we visited Larry and daughter, Emma, for 5 days. Quite a trip, scenically speaking, and a great deal of fun. The best part was seeing son and granddaughter. Carrie was visiting her own mother, most of the time. We did have fun. Bend is about 3500 feet and the weather was snowy. Natch, we went skiing (Trail skiing in the mountains). It's great sport. Among other things, you learn to glide uphill and go pretty fast downhill. Age 72 is no excuse. I'll tell you, though, if it weren't for a generous-hearted soul with a shovel who stopped by, we'd still be up there trying to push that damn car out of a slippery ditch we dug for ourselves about a foot down into the ice and dirt.

Bend is a nice town of about 50,000 souls. It used to be just a wide spot in the road when I commuted to college from Los Angeles. I'd pass through Bend and if I didn't look sharp I'd miss it. But it does have a lot of nice things about it besides snow and cold weather. Half of the disillusioned California population is migrating in that direction. If they can stand the cold weather, they say, "This is nice—let's stay a while and bring our California sophistication to these poor benighted people." So, this may become the new Los Angeles of the Pacific Northwest. Ain't we lucky?

Sorry to hear about the Carpell whatever it is. The nice thing about my typing—it never was any good—so I just bumble along and don't know the difference. Keep up the good work with your kids. They're just great people. You've done a nifty job with them. I love to see them square things around and pull together so well. You remind me more and more of the grandmother we both adored.

I'm glad to see you recognize I'm older than you. Sometimes I worry a bit that you're catching up.

Love you.
T

In March, Aunt Sarah sends a postcard to Dad that describes a reunion she had with her grandchildren, Sadie's boys.

Sarah's Postcard to Dad – March 5, 1996

A postcard with an aerial view of **Courthouse** and **Cathedral**

Rocks, Entitled "Red Rocks of Sedona".

We visited this magnificent place Sunday—a 2 hr. drive from Phoenix. Weather perfect—Roads great. My trip out here was a piece of cake. We have made easy meals: salmon salad & Turkey salad sandwiches—washed down with margaritas & chilled wine—smiley face. The two boys are giants – 6'2" & 6'4". The older boy is a terrific host. We took a 4 mile hike up some foothills—and we have had a lot of laughs. Sadie is relishing every minute with her boys.

A memorable trip for all—Love, Sarah

LETTERS FROM TRAVIS

Immediately, Dad responds to Aunt Sarah after he receives the postcard from Sedona. This causes him to start dreaming about trips he would like to take someday.

March 9, 1996

Dearest Sarah:

Thanks for the enthusiastic card from Sedona. You're right—magnificent is the only way to describe that place. Your letter was a tonic because I knew it was so important for Sadie to have a close contact with her boys. It will be a medicine like no other and do them all a world of good—including yourself. Like you we were overwhelmed with Sedona and its magnificent red cliffs. So many wonderful places to see and so little time to see it all. We've been there at least 3 times and are ready to return—first chance!

Today has been busy! We had Alva's family over for her 37th birthday celebration. Wonderful party and a wonderful daughter who is loved by them and us together. She has a jewel of a baby boy—3 months old now. He is by all odds the calmest, most adorable baby on the face of the earth. Alva is breast feeding him and intends to continue all year, I guess. That little baby didn't let out a peep in 3 hours, smiles the whole time. The older kids of course, adore him and are just great at a party with a lot of adults. Our in-laws vary a bit as one would expect, but this branch is just tops.

We're still mulling over where to head out in the world for a bit of adventure. Can't let my sister out do me in the travel department. Lucia is, of course, Irish, and that's a part of the British Isles I haven't seen. We'd like to go there, but there are so many paces competing. Ireland and the Far East, Africa.

The only places I can rule out are England, France and Germany. I don't want to fight WWII all over again. Decisions,

71

decisions!!

LATER! We had a nice birthday party for our daughter Alva last night, her 37th. Hard to realize my baby girl is now 37… I don't even think of myself as that old. But when you're in your second childhood, you're young forever.

Hope all is well with you and yours. I'll send this to your home. If you don't answer it for a year, I'll know you extended your trip.

Love,
Travis

1988 Christmas Margaret; Lake Forest Park

LETTERS FROM TRAVIS

In July, Dad raves about Aunt Sarah's daughter, Sadie and her family. He is impressed with her ability to work at a high school with twice as many students as he had during the years he was an administrator. Her young daughter, husband, Jon, and his mother who lived in the area were with Sadie.

July 3, 1996

Dearest Sarah:

Your daughter, Sadie, her husband Jon and their little girl plus Jon's mother stopped in for a visit today. You remember that we stayed with them in Anchorage for over a week. Sadie has always been most cordial to us and this get-together was no less so. I think our common bond is probably helped by the fact that we were both high school counselors. Sadie works in a high school of more than 2400—very large as high schools go. I worked at Roosevelt in Seattle as vice principal, one of Seattle's largest and best schools and it was only a school of 1800 students most of the time I was there. She has a lot of responsibility and I admire her professionalism on the job as well as her happy disposition and lovely personality. She comes by it honestly—inherited from her mother.

Lucia and I are definitely going on a trip somewhere— the question is where? We thought of Russia, Ireland, Costa Rica or Canada, but every one we check into seems to have some drawback—mostly money! Say, you wouldn't want to go with us, would you? If we went to Ireland we could stop by and pick you up in, say New York and make it a threesome.

Wouldn't that be a ball? I know you love to travel and money is no object—or at least as far as you're concerned. And as for me—Heck! You can't take it with you, and if I wait to much longer I may not be able to see the sights too well.

MEMORIES AND FORGETFULNESS

Think about it!

I understand, Ben, Anna's husband isn't having all that much good luck. We hope Anna holds up O.K. and that he recovers his good health in good shape.

Love to you. Don't work too hard with your grandchild! Keep in touch.

Travis

A few days later, Dad writes to Aunt Sarah again. He and my mother are planning on receiving a visit from her youngest daughter, Anna. She visits and seems to be on top of the world while living in Chicago and is thinking about buying a house there. Dad quips about playing golf and forgetting the scores.

July 8, 1996

Dearest Sarah:

Two days ago we had a visit from Sadie, her husband and mother-in-law and the baby. Today we hope to see Anna. She is due at any minute. I really feel flattered that my nieces want to make a special effort to see their uncle. You have two marvelous daughters. I love them dearly and I know their special attention is a reflection of our own close relationship over the years. You've set a great example for them over the years and I flatter myself that our own close relationship has set an example for them as well.

LETTERS FROM TRAVIS

We had a great visit with Sadie. She wants to come back to the lower 48, but doesn't know for sure when they will release her from the school district. You probably have more up to date information than I do, but she was pretty vague about it when I asked her.

Later:-Anna has now dropped in for a visit with us. She seemed to be on top of the world—enthusiastic about Chicago—in fact she's talking about getting a house there even though she and Ben might not stay for more than a couple of years. Alva brought over her 7-month-old and they compared notes. The two girls are cute to watch. I think we're both lucky!

Lucia and I are contemplating a trip overseas this summer. We've already turned down one opportunity to go on a kind of religious mission to Russia. But we're still looking! We're considering possibilities in Ireland and in Costa Rica… without the proselytizing requirements. Travel is getting quite expensive, but I don't think it's going to get better by waiting.

I wanted to report that we had wonderful reunions with both girls. You're a lucky mom. I'm planning a fair amount of golf these days. I purposely forget the scores (which is not hard to do) but the exercise is good.

Love you. Keep in touch.
Travis

Aunt Sarah liked Dad's next letter and wrote, "This is a keeper," on the envelope. My father's silly comments filled the letter showing off his personality. Evidently, he became enamored with my father-in-law's condominium because he called it the Taj Mahal.

MEMORIES AND FORGETFULNESS

He also comments on his niece Anna's fortitude as he described the fact that cancer has returned to her husband. Anna has met difficulties in her life with loved ones either dying or facing trials and tribulations. Anna's husband, Ben, having cancer was one of those events. Also, Dad describes, in an irreverent way, activity near Everett where eventually the local government wants to house homeless people.

August 16, 1996

Dearest Sarah:

Cats are all the same. They don't know much, but they do know that food comes from the refrigerator. They're also good psychologists too and know that persistence pays off…a constant, piteous whine will break down the firmest resistance and eventually they will eat. I really never did like cats but have to admit they're less trouble than dogs, even though I like dogs better. I used to be jealous of doctors because they make so much money and seem so wise. However, I now find out that vets make more than doctors and they don't get sued as much, and they're more like human beings and less like the Almighty which is quite comforting. So, when you talk about cats, I speak your language. I should have been a vet.

We took our granddaughter, Emma, down to see her other grandfather, Richard Ames. This business of visits is all worked out very scientifically—35.5 hours with us and 35.5 hours with the Ames grandparents… give or take a few days. I knew Richard had moved from his West Seattle house, of modest proportions, to a swank waterfront condominium overlooking the harbor and the city on the other side, since retiring from his judgeship. I wasn't prepared for anything so grand. Boy those judges must do all right! This place was an elegant palace…I felt I was entering the Taj Mahal. The cat has a bigger bedroom in their place than I do at home.

But, I don't really care. Lucia and I have our vast coterie of friends and confidents. And besides, I'm in deep contemplation over the book I'm about to write. I haven't decided on the subject or the title; But my mind is swirling with ideas, If I can only catch ahold of one of them long enough to write it down.

Sorry to hear about Ben's cancer surfacing again… and the baby being sick. Difficulties never seem to come along one at a time—but in bunches. Anna certainly seems determined to meet the challenges head-on. She's pretty impressive and obviously has a good head on her shoulders. Whatever comes, you know she'll meet it head-on and handle it well.

The other night we had all five of Mike's kids overnight. I was reminded of Moses Brown, when the visiting team stayed overnight in our dorm and half of us slept on the floor. Kids don't worry about creature comforts, fortunately. The main thing is—when do we eat?

There's a man-made island up in the Sound near Everett. For years they dredged the harbor, dumping the dirt on the side of the channel away from the city. After many years, they found they had formed a long low island of some 2 ½ miles out in the Sound. Pretty soon trees and shrubs started to grow there. I understand they are thinking of making it into a resort for indigents. They can put them out there with fishing poles and forget them. It'll solve a lot of problems: Get the bums off the street, keep them busy and contented, and provide cheap housing. Social Services countrywide will never be the same. I'm thinking of offering my services as a "bum-director".

MEMORIES AND FORGETFULNESS

Don't let my silly remarks keep you from writing.

Love your letters and you too.

Travis

CHAPTER 7 – 1997 RECOGNITION

In January 1997, Dad and Mother took a trip to The British Isles, which included Ireland. They sent this postcard to Aunt Sarah.

Travis and Lucia's Postcard to Sarah – January 29, 1997

A postcard of "LONDON" and subtitled "TOWER BRIDGE". Date stamped ROYAL MAIL CUSTOMER SERVICES, TWICKENHAM GREAT BRITIAN

Dearest Sarah:

      Ireland is fantastic a picture-book wonderland of great beauty. They love Americans and treat us with great affection: There is, however, a lot of political unrest, so the climate is not entirely benign. Our trip has been all too short. We'll be coming back.

Love,

T & L

MEMORIES AND FORGETFULNESS

When my dear father left for Europe with my mother, sister and brother-in-law, I remember my sister returning from the trip and saying "Seeing Dad and Mother off to Ireland from England was like sending your kids away to school." She wondered if they would be okay and have a good time. Evidently, they did.

In 1997, this next letter indicates that Dad was aware of his forgetfulness, and possibly *the disease*. I didn't learn of his memory loss until 1999. Dad writes the following letter to Aunt Sarah when they return and he recounts the trip.

Feb. 18, 1997

Dearest Sarah:

Glad to hear you're going to use letter writing more often. It's not only cheaper, but in some ways more communicative. You can look back over a letter and think about what it said a second time. A little slower, admittedly, but very helpful at times—particularly when you get to the age where things don't come to mind so readily.

As you probably have gathered, I'm starting to get forgetful—a real pain in the neck—something I hope you don't have a problem with—it doesn't sound as if you do. I remember Dear Nana had this trouble and Mother was not very sympathetic. Then, she, mother, wound up having a whole lot

---

of it herself later on. Well, I saw a lot of Mother in her latter years and I must say— she kept a stiff upper lip. I remember wheeling her down the corridors of the many "homes" she state at in the latter years. She would turn back to me, look up and smile and ask "Do you love me?" I would assure her that I did and she would look ahead again with a satisfied smile saying "Well, that's good!" and we both felt the little routine was very satisfying.

Support is pretty important and your letters and calls are important to Lu and me, in case you had any doubt.

Our trip to Ireland was most satisfying—a lovely place, great people and probably the most enjoyable trip I've made, particularly of late. The only difficulty was that we spent most of our time in England, a place I am quite familiar with—at least from many years ago. Since the trip was primarily meant to accompany Alva and Ted on his promotional excursion for "Funplex" we only get to stay in Ireland 4 ½ days. This is a place that a month at least is needed. That's not out of the question, but we really did feel cramped for time—there's so much we didn't get to see. Well, a taste is better than nothing, and we'll go back again. Maybe you can join us next time.

One thing we didn't do, that, on reflection, I would have also enjoyed very much, was to visit the University of Bristol. Of course, old "Jerry" (our patron professor) is now dead, and I wouldn't have known a soul now, but just moseying around, bragging about my post wartime experience there and trying to find our old digs after 50 years would have been pretty exciting.

The nice thing about England is that things don't change as much as fast as they do here. You can go back after 50 years and Buckingham Palace looks pretty much the same as it did half a century ago—the same with the "Tower of London", the "Houses of Parliament", etc. Seattle and almost any other American city, isn't recognizable after 50 years. This isn't all bad, but it's quite reassuring to go back to a place like London after nearly a lifetime and be able to say, "I remember this!"

MEMORIES AND FORGETFULNESS

Thanks for your nice letter. Yes, I agree it's fortunate to have the children we have. My kids are very busy with their own lives, but they're always cordial to old Dad and I feel very privileged—I know you do, too.

Lots of Love. Keep the letters coming!

Travis

Upon returning from Europe and settling into his normal at home routine, Dad responds right away to Aunt Sarah after she writes him. Again, he reiterates his forgetfulness and acknowledgement of his dementia.

Now, with a perception and full understanding of Irish people, he feels like he can make further comments to Aunt Sarah about Ireland because she has expressed an interest in traveling to that country. He explains the English attitude toward the Irish and how the potato famine impacted the residents of Ireland. He writes this with an element of affection for the people. When Aunt Sarah expresses an interest in wanting to see Wales, England and Ireland he goes on to discuss England as well as Scotland and his experiences there.

LETTERS FROM TRAVIS

March 1, 1997

Dearest Sarah:

Don't think that just because I write back so soon it's incumbent on you to do the same. It's just that I'm so forgetful these days that if I put a project aside for a bit it's likely to stay that way for a long, long time. I find it's better to do something while it is fresh in my mind than to put it off—it's likely to stay off indefinitely.

I was excited to hear that you're planning to go to Ireland. Our trip has been a dream for lo these many years and it fulfilled my highest expectations. First of all—the Irish love Americans. That's of course natural—half this country is related to them. But more than that, they like our style—we're not so stuffy as the English, who they aren't at all chummy with. I learned a little history about that. When the English many years ago got interested in Ireland, they thought of the Irish as an ignorant bunch of bog-trotters and no-accounts. As a consequence, dispatched them with no more compassion they would a bunch of vermin. To add to that, the potato famine nearly completed the job for the English, and the Irish have been fighting ever since to regain their dignity and self-respect.

But, everywhere we went they showed us Yanks respect—one might almost say fondness. This is rare to come by these days. And if a guy says, "Friend let me buy you a beer!" I am apt to think his is just great and buy him one back.

I wasn't aware you'd never been to the British Isles. I was, of course, stationed there for a year or more. But in those days, sightseeing wasn't a big thing—although a beer in a local pub certainly had some merit. But, I predict you're going to enjoy the trip greatly. And, by all means see Wales and Scotland. Wales—because your forebears came from there, and Scotland because it's something else unique and beautiful. Besides, I like the Scottish style and their accent. Ralph Gould and I went to several plays in London, then…it kept us out of

83

the pubs.

Bridge four times a week certainly keeps you busy. You'll be as sharp as your grandfather at that game before long. As you say, it makes you think—I guess that's why I have trouble with it.

Like you, I have a hard time realizing our kids are passing quickly through middle age. I've been standing still for a long time—it's when you start going backwards that it hurts. Keep in touch—I love to get your letters. I want to hear about your excursion to Britain.

Love,

T

Aunt Sarah responds to Dad later in March 1997 shortly after she receives his letter. Inspired by my father and mother's trip to Ireland, she and Sadie (my cousin) have nearly finalized a trip to the British Isles which includes Ireland as well. They plan to leave in July.

Aunt Sarah's Letter to Dad

Wed. Mar 19, 1997

Dearest Lucia and Travis,

I can't keep up with the date…. and as such the only reason I take a newspaper is so that I know what day of the week it is!

LETTERS FROM TRAVIS

Thank you for the latest picture of you both—you look more and more like Daddy, Travis—although I never thought you did for years.

I think my trip to the British Isles is almost finalized—Sadie is going with me—and she's undecided about her travel arrangements—whether to go with the tour travel plans or go on her own—i.e. from Anchorage to Shannon—and back home from London to Anchorage. I'm letting the tour make my travel arrangements from Dallas to Atlanta to Shannon—and return from London to Indianapolis to Dallas (Delta). I'm really looking forward to this trip. We leave July 26 and Return August 10.

Sometime in April, one of my friends from N.C. is coming through Dallas—and will spend a couple of days down here—and 1 May my former neighbor in Potomac is coming for a visit. Her husband has Parkinson's disease—pretty advanced now. He's darn near 80—and she has had full responsibility for his care. She has to have someone take care of him when she leaves. It has been pretty exhausting.

Then in May I'll probably drive up to see Anna and the children. I miss that little baby! The drive to Chicago is a snap—a little less than 900 miles. I made it in a day and a half the last time. Of course, I leave at 6:00 AM so my time was 15 hours total—I drive a 10 hour day!

All's well otherwise—I'm playing bridge 3 days a week and loving it!—The Senior Center is my home away from home—and there's a snappy group of people who go there. We have a lot of fun.

We will be touring through the southern part of Ireland—on Brendan Tours—I'll let you know how it was when I return.

Lots of love to you both.

Sarah

MEMORIES AND FORGETFULNESS

Although, my father says he is forgetful, he has planned a trip to Maine with my mother. The brave duo's plans are described in this letter written in July to Aunt Sarah. Some of Dad's cousins on his mother's side live in Maine and upper New York State. Also, he will visit his other cousins in New York City.

July 25, 1997

Dearest Sarah:

I thought you would be interested that Lucia and I have decided definitely to take a trip to Maine in the later part of September. We have a church friend who has a farmhouse in the western part of Maine—not overly far north. This lady and her husband are church friends. They inherited a large farmhouse from her parents. It's not very fancy, but will do just fine in the September weather, although Maine is pretty far north and later than that is apt to be very cold. We will have the whole house for two weeks—are you sure you wouldn't like a change of scenery—there should be plenty of room?

Having seen pictures of Dad standing over the carcass of a dead buck when I was a youngster, I feel it is important to see for myself if Maine is as romantic as he said it was. We, of course, will see Tanny and family. For most of his adult life, he has been working on a sailboat. This summer he is finally launching it. So, I guess I'll get to act as crew for Captain Tanny once again.

Think it over. If you haven't seen Tanny and are getting bored playing bridge with the girls in Dallas, maybe you'd like to join us.

Other things are going along as usual. I keep making

long lists of the "To Do" variety. I add to the list faster than I subtract from it. I quit my job as assistant church janitor when my boss got a big raise on the bases of the work I did for free. I didn't really want to get paid, but it made me mad to get neither Thanks nor recognition while the other guy got a raise. If you can't stand the heat, get out of the kitchen, I was always told…so I got out.

We're all just fine. Alva is renovating her house (our old one) and the plans are, I think, quite elaborate. We're doing nicely in our little cabin. What was good enough for A. Lincoln, suites me.

Love,

T.

Dad and Mother took the trip to Maine. They have a marvelous time and he describes the events below remembering the sequence of events, very well.

Nov. 2, 1997

Dearest Sarah:

Have I written since we returned from Maine?? I don't think so. If I have, give it the once over lightly.

Maine was great! Just what you might think—lots of small towns, big trees and a million lakes and streams. True, the Indians have just been given the top third of the state (for hunting I guess) and the locals are being pushed out by the speculators. But, there are many lovely homes on the rugged coast, and lots of New England style old beautiful homes along the estuaries and hilly by-ways that make for scenic beauty.

MEMORIES AND FORGETFULNESS

We stopped in to see our cousin Tanny and wife in their lovely home on the waters near Castine, Maine. Tanny, as you may know, has been quite ill from an intestinal problem. The day after we left he went to the hospital for a highly chancy operation. God was looking after him and he came through a difficult situation with flying colors. It is my understanding that the operation was a success and he is now on the road to recovery. I'm glad we went to see him (we cut the visit to 1 ½ hours because he needed quiet and rest for his upcoming ordeal).

The rest of our stay was about 2 weeks in the summer house of some Lake Forest Park friends who were kind enough to loan us the use of the place. We had a great time. Next time I see you ask about the trip to the top of Mt. Washington in a steam-engine Galloping Gertie that powered up a 45 degree slope in the roughest ride you'll ever endure. I'm amazed that I had the stupidity to pay $35 a piece for the darn trip. I could have walked faster! I think I lost half my hearing and two good teeth in the bargain. Well, we had some good laughs over it with our friends, the owners of the farm. I didn't dare ask them when they were going to unload this 145 acre problem and save themselves a lot of grief, but I must admit that the experience was unique and I did get to see Tanny. But, I don't think we'll ask for reservations again for a while. Home never looked so good.

Hope all is well with you and the children and grands. When you write, give me a quick take on Sadie, Bill and Anna. I'm a terrible writer, as you know (BIG ADMISSION). But, your kids are important to me. And I know that a letter asking about them will yield an encyclopedia sized answer. So go ahead—I'm asking. And if you do answer, I promise, I'll send you a full report from my end.

We think about you a lot. Wonder how you're doing and what great ventures you're dreaming of. I promise you I'll reply with my deepest inner thoughts. Well, deepest may not be exactly the right word. Random might be somewhat more accurate. Let me tell you—there was a time when "deep" was more appropriate than now. But, anyway, your thoughts are always welcome and interesting.

Love to you and the canary and whatever offspring are around.

Travis

Later in November, Dad sends another letter to Aunt Sarah describing their cousin, Tanny's, operation. Also, Dad mentions that he is upset about me moving from Bend to Salem, Oregon. He need not have worried. The Salem office where I applied decided they needed to move a water quality engineer into air quality. I was not

Nov 27, 1997

Dearest Sarah:

In general, I'm a lousy correspondent. However, I have resolved to work on doing a better job. I'll start with a letter to you today.

As I think I may have mentioned, Lucia and I went to Maine for two weeks in September. We had a wonderful time, met many nice people and stayed in a swell cabin owned by friends here in town. Maine is a nifty place to visit…albeit a bit cold as winter comes on. It's covered with lakes, but I'll be darned if I saw a single person swimming in them. In case you didn't know Tanny who went in for a third operation on his intestine, came through this time with what has been termed a successful result. I will let you know more if and when I hear complete results.

Larry, who lives in Bend, Oregon, is thinking of giving up his nice home there and moving to the west side of the state where Carrie is now teaching certain classes in what she deems a vital (to her) job. I have reservations about the wisdom of the change, but, of course, don't mention them to the people involved. Larry is well situated in an excellent job and in a place he likes. I only mention it to you because I know my doubts will go no further and if I don't tell them to someone, I'll explode.

Birthdays always escape me. If I don't remember on Jan 3rd, drop me a hint and I'll send you a card or something. Good Lord! Every time I think 70's I'm just flabbergasted. Where did all the years disappear? My main problem is I hardly have anytime left and I haven't done a tenth of the things I thought I would. Well, between the two of us we've increased the population by 7. (directly—and a lot more in the 3rd generation). That, for good or whatever, simply has to be considered an accomplishment. I refuse to spend the rest of my days moaning about "what if".

Keep in touch—play lots of bridge and don't let yourself slow down. I'm going to do the same—except substitute "golf" for "bridge".

Love you,

Travis

moving anywhere at that time.

LETTERS FROM TRAVIS

CHAPTER 8 – 1998 UNORGANIZED

In 1998 and beyond, Mother begins to write Aunt Sarah. It is likely that by doing this, she prompted Dad to continue writing letters to his sister. She provided Aunt Sarah with information about her brother and his family. Dad had a phone call with Aunt Sarah, that allowed Mother to visit with her sister's family in California.

Mother's Letter to Aunt Sarah

Jan. 26, 1998

Dear Sarah,

Tonight we look at the story of Ireland and its famine in 1844-6 on public T.V. Some sad days when the fungus made the fields of potatoes black.

Thanks to you for phoning Travis, which he so enjoyed, and the children keeping him busy last weekend, I could be assured he was OK, allowing me to enjoy a visit with my sister and her family in California—my niece and her fiancé planned a pretty wedding in white and deep green.

Later, I phoned your and Travis' cousin, Rich, while in San Diego who now lives there—I left a message, but he did not call back. He has visited at my sister's home when our nephew Bill, Travis and I were there a few years ago.

MEMORIES AND FORGETFULNESS

Your letter arrived yesterday (Sat.), I guess, and we appreciate your love and experiences about our dear Alva and her husband, Ted. We frequently think of you and your dear Anna and her cares and her love for her little boys, yet her caring and capable ways for all of us as well.

Our frozen apples have been in the freezer until yesterday, so tonight I used a yellow cake mix and made an apple upside down cake. It smells good—cooling til tomorrow.

Lots of love for you.

Lucia

In a letter written to Aunt Sarah in March 1998, Dad discusses his son (yours truly), and then laments quitting teaching so soon. He realizes that working kept him alert for a long period of time as he faced challenges on the job. He has good memories of his experiences in education. In his own way, Dad encourages Aunt Sarah to persuade Anna to move to Texas.

March 5, 1998

Dearest Sarah:

Writing that date scares me a little. It reminds me of how close we are to the millennium. My God! Where has all the time flown? I still think I'm in the '40's or '50's I guess. I haven't moved with the times—psychologically. I have a son who is nearly 50 and I still think of him as a boy.

He's smarter than heck! My problem is he's passing me up—or I'm moving backwards. I should never have left teaching when I did. It kept me on the ball and was a continual challenge. I gave it up for the lure of the buck—and that was a bad move. I never made the bucks I thought I would, and as I look back the challenge of the job kept me on the ball and kidded me into thinking I was doing something useful. The men in our family like to talk and pretend other people are listening. I always thought Dad would have made a good teacher. I learned that in teaching you have to be careful that your ego doesn't get in your way. Self-assurance—yes.

But braggadocio doesn't make the grade. I flatter myself that I hit a good middle ground. And I loved teaching the adults at the technical school—the best four years of my educational career. Most educators say that being a vice-principal is a terrible job. But, I had that distinction for 13 years and enjoyed it very much. The youthful miscreants didn't seem to want to test me out (a lucky thing) and the principal's I worked for left me pretty much alone, which must have meant they were, in general, satisfied. As I look back, those were pretty good years… not much money in them, but who cares—the memories are good.

In your letter you discuss Anna's plans and whether she'll return to Texas. I would think that it would really be a ball for you if she would stay with you for a while in Texas. That big house needs another person and I'll bet you two would enjoy being there together—you with your senior's group and Anna with her family concerns. Chicago may be a great place, but that big house of yours is just crying out for some people to live in it.

Keep in touch. Lucia sends her love. I look up on the wall where Mother and Dad look back. They send their love, also.

Love,

T.

MEMORIES AND FORGETFULNESS

In April 1998, Dad and Mother send Aunt Sarah a card wishing her Happy Easter. First, Mother references Dad's cousin, Rich's, call to Dad. Then, Dad also mentions the call and says it reminds him to keep in touch with family.

Mother and Dad's Note to Jane

On a card that states "With Best Wishes" Inside "Just want to say—You're wished a world of happiness… Today, tomorrow and always!"

April 8, 1998

Happy Easter, Sarah

Thank you for your Saturday phone visit. Last Thursday in response to my phone call, your cousin, in San Diego, called to visit with Travis. He tells me your cousin is fine and working.

Lucia

Great to talk with you the other day. You sounded tip top—a description I don't always apply to myself these days. Talking with cousin Rich, reminded me that I've got to keep in touch with the relatives better. I may have told you that the last 4 or 5 times we've been in San Diego, I've tried very hard to contact him with no luck. This was a real break-through and I hope to keep the contact going.

Happy Easter—lots of love, Sis!

T&L

LETTERS FROM TRAVIS

In May, Dad writes Aunt Sarah. He is troubled by the date and how close it is to the millennium. He marvels at his children making their way in the fast paced world and extolls his wife for putting up with his senseless ways. He discusses the fledgling city of Lake Forest Park and some of the characters associated with city government. When he realizes the low-spirited nature of the letter he changes it to more of an upbeat tone about his family.

Dad's Letter to Sarah

May 2, 1998

Dearest Sarah:

Every time I write the above date I get a bit startled—My God, we're coming to the new millennium, faster than scat. We were talking at dinner about how fast things are moving these days—and the date is moving a lot faster than I like. At nearly 75, I'm getting very sensitive about time and how fast it moves.

Well, at least our children are holding their own well in a fast moving world. Our children are all doing great and hanging in there through good and bad, and my little wife is my strength and salvation. She puts up with my dopy ways—I don't know how.

I was at the dentist yesterday. He did a fourth filling in one tooth. I asked him how he could get four fillings in one tooth—and he said it wasn't easy. But, the alternative was to

---

pull the tooth and put in a false one. We both agreed we'd hold off on that one as long as possible.

I think my house is gradually sliding down the hill it's clinging to. I notice the doors aren't closing easily and I have to keep sanding down the parts that stick. Well, I figure if the house will just hang in there a few more years, it'll be someone else's worry.

We're getting a new city government in Lake Forest Park. I suppose that includes fancy taxes as well. Some of my friends are on the city council. I try to get very friendly with them, but after I vote for them, they get awfully business-like and distant. One guy who I actually went door to door campaigning for is now too busy to see me.

We've had a long siege of El Nino's presence in this part of the world. It has been raining regularly for months now and we're wondering if the same patter will hold all summer. I thought for a while it was just the media trying to put a sensational spin to the weather prognostication. But, this pattern of wet weather has been going on for months and seems inclined to keep on forever. I generally can take the weather—good or bad—but this is getting pretty tiresome now.

As I read this over it seems a bit on the gloomy side. Actually, except for the weather, things are going well with us. Alva's brood is growing and maturing. They are a swell bunch and those young parents are getting them off to a great start. My daughter, if I do say so, has gotten her youngsters off on the right track—considerate, happy, energetic and talented. Even the baby, at 2 ½, knows who the head honcho is. I have him saluting now.

Keep in touch. We, 70 year-olds, have to stick together. If we don't the youth will grab the ball and run with it.

Love,

Travis and Lucia

LETTERS FROM TRAVIS

Aunt Sarah calls Dad and they have a nice discussion. Dad follows up with a letter, and in jest, he says my mother has another guy in their lives. Evidently, Mother has been on the computer "on-line." The letter is truncated and rather short.

Dad's Letter to Sarah Draft

June 1, 1998

Dearest Sarah:

Nice to talk with you yesterday. Thanks for the call.

We have another person in our lives. I never realized a computer could be such a living presence. Lucia is fascinated with "on line", a new personality in our lives that I don't know very well. I guess I'm a bit jealous, but I'll try to put the new guy in perspective. He's only a machine, but I have a hard time competing with him—it's a challenge.

(Note: The rest of the letter is missing)

To clarify, Mother writes a letter to Aunt Sarah discussing the word processer she had been using. She is also using email. She responds after Dad has received a nice letter from Aunt Sarah. She tells Aunt Sarah that Dad is working on a 1000 piece jigsaw puzzle and they had a nice trip to Leavenworth, WA. She was happy that their grandson, Tom, was able to fix Dad's camera.

Mother's Letter to Sarah   June 15, 1998

Dear Sarah,

This word processor works better than the typewriter because the typist can make corrections before the final copy is made all at once by pressing the code and print keys.

T'was so nice to get your letter which Travis just read to me. You mentioned the telephone and e-mail replacing letters. Well, you are right about that. I wanted to E mail on the internet so badly and now I have it I don't turn it on that often. Yet, I learned that 'You have mail' came on—with sound— even, when I chanced to turn it on last week and found a little brother from Tucson, had written me and Travis where it was only 85 degrees and his wife was better that day. Without addressing an envelope or stamping an envelope I popped off a few lines and Travis pushed the mouse to 'send' and off it went to my brother and his spouse.

Well our patterns of living have changed to get used to this new communication, and it is a lot of 'Learnin' to figure it all out.

With Love,

Lucia

Hi again—It is 7-2-98 and your brother is content to spend his spare time on that 1000 piece puzzle. Today when I made a plan with Tom to help us with yard work (right after his

---

orthodontist appointment in Lake Forest Park) he was with Grandpa for a couple hours and had had lunch before I got home from A.D. Center. I saw what was pruned and tossed out. (This is Thursday when I assist in the water exercise program in Bothell and then help serve lunch, so I get free lunch.)

I love working with Mike's oldest, Tom. He runs to the garage for saws, rakes, pruners, and broom, while I tug away at ground covers filling up any would-be paths. He hauls the wheelbarrow down the hill—steep one—like a pro and puts stuff where Grandpa told him.

Then, I get to visit with him about cameras. Actually he got T's camera working. Don't know if T. has any interest in it at all, because he'll say okay, take along yours, Lucia. We had a nice trip to a Germantown over the Stevens pass at 4,061 feet to Leavenworth. Three days we stayed in a cabin with Alva and three precious children---all but T. went into the pool which is only a block away. And the speed limit is 15 mph so children could ride bikes along the road. We may go over to the cabin again this summer. I must enclose a snapshot or two.

We are both "healthy", eat well and have energy for each day!!

Much love to you and yours

Lucia

In August, Dad explains the need to repair the condo he had rented. He announces that my sister Alva and her family are moving to Denver.

MEMORIES AND FORGETFULNESS

August 26, 1998

Dearest Sarah:

I never know quite where you are at any one time—such a gad-a-bout. With me—I'm either eating or asleep. Once in a while I go to the store. Well, a simple life is a good life—I guess. My greatest ambition is to play more golf. I'll write you at your home. That way I know you'll get it eventually.

We're stay-at-home—mostly. For one thing the duplex has undergone extensive renovation—not only costly, but time-consuming. One of the guys who lived there bought himself a new home and left the apartment in sad need of repairs. I was almost glad he left. It gave us a chance to renovate it from top to bottom. It looks great now. Newly painted, new carpets throughout—everything clean and shipshape.

Alva and family have left for their new home in Denver. They have a nice new home outside of Denver. We'll visit them after they get well settled. We'll miss the children. They have been a great joy to me and things won't be quite the same without them nearby. Ted, her husband, has the job of heading up a much larger recreation program. It should work out well. He knows the business. Alva has been working as his secretary for some time in Seattle. I don't believe she will be doing that in Denver. Ted put their home (our old one) in tip top shape. I hope it sells relatively soon. It is on the market already.

Hope all is well with you and your scattered family.

Love to all,
Travis and Lucia

Probably, in September, Aunt Sarah writes my

father, although the first page of the letter is missing. Among other things, she describes going through their mother's papers and miscellaneous possessions. Some of her mother's photos are from Rockport and they create warm memories of her at that time.

Sarah's 2nd half of a Letter to Dad – Likely first of September

I went through Mother's "papers" financial records, etc. which I tossed—and the photo albums which I went through, took some pictures out—so my kids know where we come from and what we looked like growing up, and I'm sending you the albums so your kids know the same. The later albums are mostly Rockport and Seattle pictures which you would like to share with your kids. Then there are some bookplate things of Dad's that I think might someday be very valuable to collectors—Bookplate Society publications in pristine condition dating back to 1904!—Don't throw them away. One of your sons might be very interested in having those (watch the "Antique Show" on Public Television) you never know what treasure lurks in your attic!

Well, that about does it from this part of the world. I know you are about as active as I am even though Alva and Ted are gone and you still have a few grandchildren left in the area. I hope all is going well with Alva and Ted in Colorado. Send me their address next time you write. Lots of love to you both—and a ton of good birthday wishes

Love,

Sarah

MEMORIES AND FORGETFULNESS

When I opening this next letter, I found a card with a frazzled lady sitting in a big chair with a quill pen writing a letter on a desk filled with books, letters, paint brushes, half eaten sandwiches, a glass of wine and other odds and ends. Then, inside the card I find the phrase "Just as soon as I get organized…" and a letter from Dad to Aunt Sarah. It was written one day after my father's 75th birthday. Most definitely, he has not lost his sense of humor about himself. I think it is a funny way of saying he does not feel organized, mentally or physically.

September 10, 1998

Dear Sarah;

This problem, "identified by the enclosed card", applies to most of us, but particularly to the male gender in our house. I haven't been organized for years and even when I was young and more alert, I wasn't all that well organized. This is a tough situation for teachers especially. But my students never brought it to my attention. After all, the person who decides on the grades to be given does have a certain amount of leverage. My teaching style dealt with generalities more than specifics, which may not have been such a wonderful learning situation, but did give the teacher a certain "other world" mystique which may have been impressive with some of the students anyway.

I'm presuming you're back home by now and playing cards daily with "the girls". Lucia spends a couple of days per week at the so-called "Senior Center" where she leads a group of elderly people to whom she gives solace and affection. She is very good at doing this and loves doing it. I on the other hand, would rather play golf then lead elderly seniors in group activities and I rarely go to the Senior Center. I did take a painting class there once, but found that I don't follow in Dad's artistic footsteps and gave it up. Since then, the cost has risen substantially, so I have a double reason to avoid the activity.

Daughter Alva and family have moved to Denver, where Ted had a leadership role in directing a recreational center much like the one he ran here in Seattle, but much larger and more challenging. They have moved lock stock and barrel, so we shall no longer see them regularly. Denver's a long way off.

Hope you're enjoying your life back home. We're looking forward to hearing all about it.

Love

Travis and Lucia

In her next letter, Aunt Sarah explains that Anna has decided to move to Keene, New Hampshire. She tries to reconcile the move but admits she will miss her two grandsons terribly. Ultimately, Aunt Sarah decides that she can fly and rent a car to see her youngest daughter and grandsons.

Sarah 's Letter to Dad

Sept. 27, 1998

Dearest Travis:

I have just been listening to a TV sermon by the

minister of the United Methodist Church of Dallas… I feel better—so then I read the Sunday paper—I feel worse.

Nothing much new here—Anna has decided that she wants to live in Keene, New Hampshire. She went to visit a very dear friend of hers who lives in NH and she fell in love with the area—made and offer on a house in Keene, which backs up to a preserve—has 2 acres. The owner was a builder—it has solar panels (auxiliary to an oil furnace) and 2 colleges in Keene. Antioch and Keene State—and she thinks that this will be a good environment in which to bring up 2 boys. Well, I can't dispute that…except she'll be so FAR AWAY! Anyway, I shall trust in the Lord and her good judgement and my ability to <u>butt out</u>. But I'll miss my two little boys.😵

She closes on the sale of her house on the 29th of October and leaves bag and baggage and two little boys loaded up in the car for Keene—of course, all this is contingent on the SALE of her house going through without a hitch. They leave on closing day for New Hampshire. It's not a 2 day drive from here to Keene. I guess, if I want to see them, I'll be flying into Springfield Mass and renting a car and driving into Keene.

Hope all is going well with you two—I know how much you must miss Alva and Ted and the children—But, you've been lucky to have had most of your grandchildren close by for so long.

I started experimenting with quilting. It's a lot more difficult and "precise" than it looks. But, I'm going to struggle til I master the art.

Lots of Love to you both,

Sarah 👧

LETTERS FROM TRAVIS

This next letter has no signature. Likely, it was a draft, and may not have been sent, completed or both. Dad starts his letter that was written in October by describing the sale of Alva's house and now that the home has sold he and Lucia need to figure out their portion of the proceeds because they had a contract with Alva and Ted. He knows his decision making is not as strong as it used to be because he is suffering with dementia. He is worried that he will make "dumb" decisions. Also, he realizes that his dementia places a strain on my mother to "fill in the gaps." Additionally, Dad relays a story about the neighbor who just got back from a reunion of WWII vets. He explains he doesn't have these reunions because his outfit never stayed in one place after the war.

Oct. 21, 1998

Dearest Sarah:

We're deep in the foggy depths of analyzing the problems of who gets what in the transfer of our old house in Bothell to a new person who has bought it from Alva and Ted, who were buying it from us. All very complicated and the road filled with potholes if you're not careful.

I'm not thinking as clearly as I used to and I tend to back off from decisions that may turn out to be dumb on later evaluation. Fine for me to use this excuse but tough on Lucia who has to fill in the gaps. With Alva and Ted now in Denver, communication by long distance is sometimes a little less than easy.

Winter has now set in for real. In Seattle that means plenty of rain (and later on snow). We haven't gone anywhere. We keep talking about it but never quite get to the point where we take off. If I didn't have to go to the doctor once in a while—I'd never get out of my easy chair.

One of the activities that many of the WWII guys enjoy is the yearly get-together of the WWII reunions. My long-time neighbor and friend Bob Barnes just got back from his yearly bash. Unfortunately the Air Corps pushed the guys around so much, they never stayed in one place long enough to get organized. None of my outfits stayed in one place long enough to make permanent contacts—therefore no reunion.

In a letter written in late October, Aunt Sarah discusses her storage unit business in Tyler, Texas and eventually selling her place. She is working on the kitchen cabinets and trying to fix the house in anticipation that she might move. Although Aunt Sarah is not in a hurry, she tries to figure out a good place to move. She considers several locations that are near her children, but wonders if her body could tolerate the colder climate. Possibly, she could just stay in Dallas at a senior living center where planned activities occur. Aunt Sarah feels that she is suited to this environment from years of living in a military compound.

Sarah's letter to Mother and Dad

Pardon the "editing"   October 25, 1998

Dearest Lucia and Travis-

It is Sunday AM 6:00—still dark—in spite of the time change—and it brings back memories of the three years I drove down to Tyler (to the mini-warehouse) leaving Dallas at 6:00 AM so that I would get there by 7:45. I did that every Monday and usually came home in the dark. It was 106 miles----That was after Will died and I ran that place until I sold it. How time flies. He and Mother both died in 1993—Mother March 17 and Will in September. Sounds like I dwell on the past—but far from it—I live in the present, welcome change and think about, and plan for, the future!

Right now I am refinishing kitchen cabinets—I have been working on those a few at a time—sanding, re-staining and then giving them 3 coats of polyurethane. It is not a quickie job like painting, but I enjoy working on wood, and I had a good teacher in Will. Each of our children, Bill, Sadie and Anna, inherited that love of woodworking, and of course Sadie married a master craftsman in Jon.

Anyway, all of this refinishing is in anticipation of eventually selling this house. I don't want to have to do it all in a hurry. When I finally take the "plunge"—then the question will be—where will I go!—to Montana (brrrr) where Sadie and

---

MEMORIES AND FORGETFULNESS

Jon will eventually live—to New Hampshire near Anna another chilly spot for an old lady—or to Birmingham where Bill and Mindy are—but with Bill still working, there could be a job transfer—and then I'd be stuck! The solution might be to stay here in Dallas—in a Senior citizen type place—which would be like "Leisure World" in Maryland (and around the country) which has duplexes which you buy and medical facilities if needed—transportation if needed, but you can live independently as long as you want—or can. And the beauty of that type of living environment is that you have a built in social life with other seniors, activities in a central location (mine would be bridge) and trips planned just like your local Senior Center—I can't think of a pleasanter cocoon! Does it sound suffocating to you? Well, having dwelled for years in "planned military communities" I'm quite used to this sort of environment.

Right now, I'm thinking this is probably a good time (in the next couple of years) to make that sort of move—while I'm still healthy and able to handle the downsizing that would have to take place—whew, what a job!

Anna sold her house in Chicago—(Perhaps I already mentioned that in previous letters). They close on October 29th—she has purchased a house in New Hampshire—(Keene)—small town—the house is on 2 acres with a pond—backs up to a forest preserve. The house was built by a builder for himself, whose brother was the architect. It has solar panels on the roof, 2X6 studs with 6 inches of insulation all around, 2300 sq. ft., 2 car garage with lots of built-ins, 18 years old, and in the top 5% of "well built" houses according to the building inspector. Anna wants to bring the boys up in a small town, in the North where she feels schools are better. She and the two little boys are flying back there on Oct 29th and a friend is driving her car back for her.

Whereas my drive to Chicago from Dallas (I've done it

7 times) was a snap, only 900 miles, 15 hours, I won't be driving to New Hampshire from Dallas. My kids are so far away—and probably will remain so.

I'm spending Thanksgiving with Bill and Mindy. I'll drive; it's a quick 2 day trip—one day if you want to drive 13 hours. Then in July (1999) I'm going to visit Sadie. Sometime between now and then I'll make that trip to New Hampshire— by plane!

Meanwhile, I'll probably just stay here in Dallas until I'm 1) physically disabled or 2) mentally incapacitated!!!

Glad to hear you are still in good voice, Travis—I sound like a rusty wheel—but I love my classical CD's so I still have music in the house—and we have a classical music station on the radio which I flick on daily! That and bridge and maintaining this house and yard keeps me <u>busy</u>.

Take care of yourselves—I know you miss Alva and family—I feel the same way about Anna now that I can't hop in the car and get to her and the boys in 2 days.

Lots of love to you both—

Sarah and Gypie

Dad composes a letter emphasizing Lake Forest Park and describes the local city government. He reminisces about his grandmother (mother's mother) coming to rescue his family of origin during The Depression.

MEMORIES AND FORGETFULNESS

Nov. 7, 1998

Dearest Sarah:

I think I'm now 2 letters behind so I better get cracking! But that's routine. I'm behind in my yard work, behind in my dental appointments and generally behind the eight ball. But, at least it's not like it used to be when we were young and we owed everybody on the east coast. Grandmother came to our rescue and it's a good thing she was a New Englander and a saver or we'd all have wound up in hock up to our elbows. But, I'm glad in a way that I was brought up in The Depression. You and I learned to pay our bills and that makes life a whole lot simpler.

About the change noted above. Lake Forest Park is really pretty small but we <u>think</u> big. The problem is—people are pouring into this area and soon it will be nothing but condos and honking traffic. Cars going in any direction waiting in long lines of traffic—and the accident rate is increasing. Our scenic view will soon be rows and rows of brick buildings and the lake will probably be paved over.

Alva and Ted keep us pretty well informed about life in Denver. They have a nice place in the suburbs and seem to like it very much. They're going to see us next month and we'll probably be deluged with pictures. They sold their renovated Lake Forest Park house. If I'd been a little younger, I think I'd have bought it back…it's <u>very</u> nice, now.

Hope everything works out well in your long-delayed departure from your old home. I have a sneaking hunch, however, that won't happen tomorrow.

Love you!

T.

LETTERS FROM TRAVIS

Aunt Sarah responds to the previous letter by telling my father about her family, the trips for Thanksgiving to Bill and Mindy (her son and daughter-in law) and seeing Anna as well as her boys. Aunt Sarah notices her changing health situation and speculates on her longevity. I do not know if she wants to make Dad feel better or if this is a genuine complaint. I do not remember my Aunt complaining much yet she appears to be very candid with her brother. She philosophizes about crowded cities and addresses increases in population. The most telling sentence lets us know that she saved all Dads letters for posterity; presumably so we could all enjoy them.

Nov. Dec.
Nov 30, 1998! 5:30AM

Dearest Travis,

I've lost all track of time (dates, that is) see Above!

I just returned from Birmingham where I spent the Thanksgiving week with Bill and Mindy—I drove, of course. Left Dallas on Sunday, Nov 22—and took 2 days to get there— It's really only a day and a half drive—about 10-11 hours—but I didn't want to push it and arrive exhausted. But coming home I made it in one day—11 hours. It was beautiful weather both coming and going. We're in the 70's down here. It's really only a day and a half drive—about 10-11 hours—but I didn't want to push it and arrive exhausted. But coming home I made it in one

---

day—11 hours. It was beautiful weather both coming and going. We're in the 70's down here. Highly unusual thanks to "La Niña". They say we're going to have a warm, DRY winter—which is a bad sign for crops and the bugs won't die off-ugh!

Bill and Mindy's home is beautiful. She inherited some gorgeous antiques (furniture, etc.) from her family—a bed in the guest room similar to the enclosed picture—Doesn't that remind you of Mother and Dad's bed back in Hingham? Mindy wanted some new valances for their bedroom so we shopped for material and they put grandma to work making "swags and cascades" for their two bedroom windows. Bill is quite a good cook and in between shopping and measuring, he managed to make 2 loaves of cranberry bread, cranberry relish and stuffing for the turkey! Downstairs in their basement, he has a workshop that he would be the envy of "Norm" on "New England Woodshop"—or whatever that program on PBS is called! He just finished a large hope chest for his daughter, made a dolls cradle for his niece—makes wooden bowls out of interesting fruit woods. I brought 3 big peach tree logs down to him from my 20 year old peach tree which was more trouble than the peaches were worth, so I cut it down! The birds and the squirrels got them before I could and for the past several years all I've been doing was picking up half eaten peaches off the lawn every morning—anyway. It was a pleasant week in Birmingham—Mindy is a dear and Bill so thoughtful.

I'm leaving for New Hampshire on Saturday, Dec 5th— (next Sat.) to see Anna and my boys—I feel they're "mine"; I've taken care of them for so long and have been in Chicago with them almost longer than I've been at home this past year! I'll only stay a week, but I wanted to see them again—flying this time.

As far as your weight… I notice that in my advancing years I don't have the appetite I used to have—plus I don't eat the fattening foods that we used to—Do you suppose your weight loss is due to similar reasons? Also, we drop muscle weight which we used to have—I'll tell you what has happened to me—I used to be 5' 2"!!! I kept wondering why my slacks were dragging on the ground! It's the cartilage between the back bones which is thinning (disappearing, I guess)—My fingers are getting crooked like grandmother's—and my hair—well, you know how thin Mother's was—well "DITTO"!

However, to look on the bright side, my blood pressure is 120 over 80—I'm never sick other than my one cold a year, usually in January—All my contemporaries are taking pills every four hours for all kinds of illnesses—and all I take is Calcium. If I don't get struck by lightning, I'll probably live til I'm 91+ (that thought terrifies me).

Anyway, you're right about our crowded cities—traffic is unbelievable—all day, not just at rush hour. Instead of widening streets and trying to produce more food (ADM's advertisement on TV) we should be reducing the population world wide—we are out pacing the ability of the planet's resources to sustain us at the rate we're procreating. I've said this for YEARS—when I saw the rat demonstration in a cage. And we wonder why the elevation of crime, road rage, psycho's and disease??? "Nuff said—I'll get of my soap box.

It's fun getting your letters. I have saved all of your letters for posterity, and one of these days I'll ship them out to you along with Mother's photo albums and some other things that your kids should have.
Lots of love to you all—

Sarah

MEMORIES AND FORGETFULNESS

CHAPTER 9 – 1999 - 2000 MOTIVATION

In 1999 and 2000, my father writes fewer letters. By this time he has told me that he has been diagnosed with dementia. Book Two describes my reaction after hearing that he has this devastating disease. Still, Aunt Sarah continues to write even though Dad writes less. She continues to provide insight into her family and compares notes to what happens in my family of origin; my father's family. She continues to provide insight into her family and compares notes to what happens in my family of origin; my father's family.

Sarah's Letter to Travis – possibly 1999

(First part of the letter is missing)

      Bill is in the process of interviewing for another job. He sees his present job as having no future upward mobility—difficult decision, as this would mean a move out of Birmingham and Mindy has never lived anyplace else. Her whole family is in Birmingham, and it will be difficult for her to leave. You and I don't understand that, having been uprooted so many times—a move to me means a great time to clean house and get rid of things and an exciting new beginning. This is the longest I've lived anyplace!

MEMORIES AND FORGETFULNESS

Sadie and Jon will leave Alaska in 2 years and take up residence in Montana, about 35 miles north of Missoula where Jon has some property, and it is country that Jon loves. He'll set up his wood working business there. He's a master craftsman. Sadie will probably do something with the University in Missoula, but initially she'll help Jon market his products, and maybe set up a business of her own. Sounds intriguing.

Anna has her hands full with 2 kids an 8 week old Labrador retriever, a paranoid cat and a 5 bedroom house to take care of and sell. Sadie is coming down in March during her spring vacation. I'll go back then—We'll probably be able to help her clean things up. She's got to have the house in good condition to show—Not easy! You two take good care of yourselves. I'm glad you have most of your kids nearby.

Lots of love to you all.

Sarah

On rereading this letter, it sounds like I'm racing the clock! Actually I probably am—and always have been. I spend my days crossing things off a "To Do" list like there's no tomorrow—and sometimes I'm glad I did it "yesterday"—and that's how I spend my life—but it doesn't mean that I'm not thinking of you frequently and lovingly. You both are very dear, and you live your lives in such an exemplary fashion, brought your children up with fine values.

They are as proud of you—as you are of them.

So again, with much love—and admiration—your somewhat wistful sister!

Aunt Sarah responds to my parents and discusses

being nostalgic as she remembers traveling through beautiful old New England; especially Keene, New Hampshire.

Aunt Sarah's letter to Lu and Travis – Feb 2, 1999

Feb 2, 1999

Dearest Lucia and Travis-

I enjoyed both of your letters, yours for the update health-wise, Lucia and Travis, for the bit of nostalgia we too frequently overlook in our hurry up, watch-the-clock, finish-the-to-do-list, get-to-the-P.O. as soon as it opens, the bank-before-it-closes and pick-up-some-milk on the way home and don't forget to make that appointment for a mammogram-already a year and a half overdue—etc. etc. etc....!! However, I never fail to be grateful that I have all these things to do and, yes, when I was in New Hampshire (in December) driving through the small town of Keene—a twinge of nostalgia ran through me when I saw all the old beautiful New England homes, many restored, some not—lending such character to the town.

I had a long talk with Sadie the other day—She had just received a long letter from Alva, part of which she read to me. She is such a darling girl, bright and insightful. I know she misses the family but apparently, they love their new location, and she says Ted is so enthusiastic about his new job. Such a wonderful little family.

I stay busy with bridge 3 or 4 days a week. One of these days I'm sure I'll get tired of it-but right now it's still a challenge and the people I play duplicate with are really sharp.

MEMORIES AND FORGETFULNESS

But, I'm starting another hobby—quilting. I'm practicing now—not doing a quilt for real—just acquainting myself with all the techniques.

As much as I have sewn, I thought quilting would be a snap. Not so. It is a very precise art! Done right, that is. Sadie sent me a "How To" book—hard cover—200 pages. I'd better hurry up and learn if I'm ever going to make quilts for my grandchildren. Speaking of which, I miss my two little boys in New Hampshire. I'm afraid if I don't see them frequently my oldest (of the two) grandson will never remember me—even though I took care of him his first six months—then when he was 9-12 months and then again on and off til now. But, at three and a half he won't have much memory of Grandma. Boo-hoo!

I'm going to visit Sadie in July 1999—I come through Seattle—but only on a 4-6 hour layover—I'll let you know date and time—and hopefully you'll be able to get down to the Airport.

I won't be taking any other trips this year. I guess I've seen enough of the world for one lifetime—lived in Europe and Asia—both coasts of the continent and North and South and in the middle. Ours is a beautiful country and I couldn't even tell you which part I like the best.

Take care of yourselves—Do still keep in touch, and if you ever want to take one more short trip—hop on down her to Dallas.

Lots of love to you both.

Sarah

LETTERS FROM TRAVIS

Aunt Sarah must have received a letter from my parents that I have not seen. At this point, I believe Mother became a little worried about Dad's dementia and that he was making fewer decisions. She felt a strong desire for Dad and Aunt Sarah to have a reunion and must have urged Aunt Sarah to come to Seattle. I remember Mother stating that she needed to contact Aunt Sarah, although I did not know why.

Sarah's Letter to Travis – March 4, 1999

March 4, 1999

Dearest Travis,

Enjoyed your letter as always, and I shall rush to answer and get this in the mail this morning on the way to the Veterinarian—Taking the cat in for her shots! She's a sweet kitty—one of Anna left with me when they moved to Chicago—long haired though, which means she gets her hair balls especially in the spring. I have medicine to give her for that about once a week—It helps somewhat. Anyway, she follows me all over the house—rushes to beat me to the telephone, curls up beside me in the chair every evening, wakes me up at 5:30 every morning with her little (de-clawed) paw nudging my cheek, and understands everything I say! We're buddies! Although, I think she thinks I'm her mommy! When I went up to Chicago to help Anna during Ben's long illness, I took her with me. It was a two day trip to Chicago by car—and of course, I had to put her in the cat-carrier. She cried for the first half hour and then settled down (and was an angel!) for the rest of the trip—9 hours the first day and 6 hours the second day. Overnight in a motel where I had to enclose her in the

---

bathroom! Oh, what we do for our pets! She's almost 11 years old—so we're two old ladies!

I'm busy as usual—this is the time of year the (6) live oak trees shed their leaves as the new ones come in—I have raked about 35 big bags of those pesky leaves so far—and that's only about half of the total that will fall. But, I want to get them up off the grass. Also with our extremely dry weather, they're a fire hazard if I let them pile up. We could use some of your rain—and from the sound of it you have plenty to spare. I hope it stops next week when I come up. I'm looking forward to seeing you both. I'll be arriving Saturday March 13—on American Airlines

AA Flt 339
Arrives Seattle 1:04 p.m.

And I leave on Saturday March 20th.

So, I guess we can get caught up in our exciting lives in a week! You know we haven't seen each other since Mother died. That's 6 years—and I must warn you—I'm no spring chicken anymore. The hair is a little thinner, the wrinkles are wrinklier, and my right leg is gimpy. No one knows why. But, my blood pressure is 120 over 89—I don't know about my cholesterol—and don't care. The weather has been absolutely gorgeous this winter/spring—we'll pay for it this summer when it is predicted to be long, hot and dry! (I'll be in Alaska for 2 weeks in July—hoorah!!

Lots of love to you both—see you next week.

Sarah

After Aunt Sarah's visit to Seattle, Dad was motivated to write his sister as a way of showing his appreciation. The letter was a draft that included a part meant for Alva's family that was crossed out and was not included. The part that is not deleted explains Dad and Mother's plans to visit my sister in Colorado. They were going to travel by train. As springtime approaches, Dad anticipates golfing sometime during the summer. His gracious demeanor shows through to the end in his next letter.

March 25, 1999

Dearest Sarah:

How nice to have you with us for a nice visit. You are certainly an easy guest to have around—lots of fun and a million laughs. Also, you have an encyclopedia of a mind that retains everything, not only of the present, but of the long past. That's especially handy when I'm around, because the past is frequently quite vague, especially that of long ago—for me.

We hope your trip was a pleasant one and that you found everything at home shipshape. We haven't had much snow this year, but the snowpack in the mountains is quite heavy. There may be some records set. We have had a lot of rain this year, down here. I'm just as glad it's raining not snow, but the wet gray days get a little tiresome.

Lucia and I as you may have heard, intend to go east to see Alva and Ed. We'll go by train and probably not stay for a long visit. I think the summer is better for extended trips this time.

One nice thing about the heavy rain and relatively warm weather—the grass is very green and growing like crazy. Green grass reminds me of the golf course. I can hardly wait.

Loved having you here and hope we can make it a habit.

Love to all,

Travis

Dad acknowledges that he has not written for a long time and also recognizes his forgetfulness. But he has not lost his sense of humor. *It is the last known letter he writes to Aunt Sarah.*

Letter to Sarah around Christmas-time 2000

Dearest Sarah:

At the moment I'm supposed to listen to a rundown of "the news" from some well-meaning people. But I thought of the long dry space in my letter-writing efforts and decided that you were first on the letter-writing list. So here goes—with apologies for the long dry-spell in our contacts.

I attended a well-run program for "the retired". It's excellent, but I decided over the long dry-spell in communication must be broken—and I better do it while I'm thinking about it.

Physically I'm fine—a trim 165 lbs. with a loving wife who feeds me well and makes sure I keep out of trouble. The old memory isn't as good as it used to be, but I'm strong as an ox and can lick my weight in wildcats...pretty good for 77 years.

Lucia and I have taken some short trips on occasion. We're thinking of a longer romp, but haven't decided where just yet.

Seattle is a swell place in the winter (or summer). Very little snow and relatively mild weather in the middle of the winter. Lucia and I haven't taken many long trips, but we're determine we're going on a safari soon. The chances are we'll go out of state possibly to California.

We think of you a lot and would like to see you one of these days. Think of a time and place we could get together—it's been quite a while. I'm still pretty active physically—mentally—well that's a different story. I forget a lot and am not very active socially. I'm probably not much of a challenge to my sharp wife—but I guess that's the way the ball bounces. I do my best. As long as I'm playing tennis or mowing the lawn, I'm operating okay. When I have to do algebra, I'm not so hot. If I wasn't reminded every once in a while, I'd probably forget to take out the garbage... or for that matter go to the bathroom.

Lucia is very patient with me, but would probably tell me where to get off if it were in her nature.

If you get a chance, write me a letter now and then. I would love to hear from you. I'll try to keep my comments on a positive note. I have drawn a picture of you fishing with a fish at the end of the line to make it a "happy picture"... for me if not for the fish.

Love you

T

MEMORIES AND FORGETFULNESS

About this time, Dad's dementia has progressed, yet he could talk a "good line" and cover up his loss of memory pretty well.

Aunt Sarah responds to Dad in a letter, where only the middle page of a multiple page letter was found. She discusses her circle of friends in Texas and their health problems. I am sure there is more relevant information in the letter, but it is nice to know that she is corresponding with my father.

Sarah's Letter to Dad – Sometime in 2000

(Partial Letter – begins and ends in middle)

…It's really cutting into my bridge! I took the car in for a tune-up. It is sinful how dependent we are on our cars. I was planning on driving out to Phoenix to see Bill and Mindy when their house is finished, but with the price of gas now, I'm not so sure I want to do that.

My duplicate partner just had a triple by-pass and valve replacement—in intensive care for over a week and she had a rough time. I took a couple of meals to her and her husband when she got home—and now her husband has congestive heart failure and about 25% use of his kidneys. So they are really in bad shape. And my friend Janice Keller, whose father was in the nursing home when mother was there. (Janice and I wrote the newsletter for the nursing home) and we helped out on Friday "Happy Hour" with singing hymns. Janice played the piano and I helped the little people sing! Anyway, she had breast cancer—recovering from that completely—but then got colon cancer—and now liver cancer. She is the dearest person and we have kept in touch—having lunch every so often and her husband joins us—but this is so sad.

I'm finding that so many of my friends are having health problems—and I'm pretty fortunate. But, I have so many things I want to do. There's just so many hours in the day.

I'm working on a "sample" quilt—for practice. I want to make a quilt for each of the children.…

MEMORIES AND FORGETFULNESS

CHAPTER 10 – 2003-2006 AUNT SARAH'S LETTERS

Aunt Sarah and my Mother are doing all the corresponding now. Essentially, Dad has stopped writing letters altogether. Although, he still has good days, his mental acuities have dropped slowly. Below, is Aunt Sarah's 2003 Holiday Christmas Letter. There is an announcement in the letter with overwhelming sad news. Anna's young daughter born in 2000, died and Aunt Sarah is concerned about her two grandsons. Also, she describes her trip to Hingham, Massachusetts and Anna's graduate studies.

Sarah's Christmas Card to Mom and Dad Nov/Dec 2003

"Wishing you a bright and beautiful holiday season!"

Dearest Lucia and Travis—I'm trying to get my Christmas cards done early before I leave for Keene—in January—Yes, I'm going up again—The boys were sort of left out when their sister needed so much attention. (their 3 year old sister died.) With Anna going to school, leaving at 6 a.m. and not getting home til 6:30 p.m., there's not much time for her with them. So, I'll be there when they get home from school— and to bake cookies, and make banana bread and homemade

---

soup and baked stuffed potatoes and pancakes and French toast and bran muffins—are you hungry yet?

Well, they get hot dogs and pizza and almost no veggies—now I'm going to see that the meals are nutritious. They are sweet boys—and I adore them. And I don't have many more years to help out my family—

It was wonderful seeing Sadie—and Travis, I forgot to tell you that when we were in Keene, the girls (Sadie and Anna) said they wanted to see where you and I grew up in Hingham. So we drove the 3 ½ hours to Hingham, went south on Main Street passed the Episcopal Church, past the Hennning's house and there it was—on Main Street—only not light grey but a soft colonial yellow. We parked the car in the cemetery behind the Old Ship Church and walked back to the house—Across the street was Frank Jones' house—the Brewman's next door to ours—all the houses had historical markers on them as we walked down Main Street to Water Street where The Allens' lived and my best friend, Hank Nickels' house—all exactly as they were 67 years ago. I couldn't find Harvey Davis' house in North Hingham. That part of Town was much younger and it was hard for me to identify his or Bucky Grey's house—Anyway the owner of our old house on Main Street saw us and when we explained why we were taking pictures of the house, he invited us in and we talked for about an hour. The rooms looked so small—but nothing has changed—still only one bathroom! Remember? The same wide planked pine floors—steep stairway—I couldn't believe we lived in those small quarters.

Well, it was some adventure and took Anna away from the sadness in Keene for a while. The memorial service was beautiful. Anna was overwhelmed when all of her professors came up from Massachusetts and several of her colleagues. We had a catered reception at the house after the service and met these lovely people—were all so obviously fond of Anna. She has a 97 grade point average—is on the Dean's list and #2 in her class of 100 students. These students will all advance together for the four year course, so they become very well acquainted. The course is condensed into 2 years 8 months and she has finished ½ of the course. I am so proud of her. It's just something mothers do!

I know you will see some of your family over the holidays. Have a lovely warm one and I send my love to them and to you both.

Sarah

Aunt Sarah writes a thank you note after Christmas of 2003, lamenting the fact that her children are spread out across the country. She fondly describes their activities, discusses the fact that she has a special place for her grandchildren and was able to bond with each one of them. She comments about my father's laugh over the phone from a recent conversation they had and says it

Thank you note from Sarah to Mom and Dad – Dec. 27, 2003

Dearest Lucia and Travis—

It was fun, as always, talking to you both—makes me wish we all weren't so far apart. But, it seems my family has always been in the far corners of the country—except for the short time when Anna and Ben lived here in Texas when they were first married. But now with Sadie and Jon in Montana—Bill in Phoenix and Anna in N.H. and you all in Seattle—we're lucky to see each other once a year! Anyway, we have the phone, thank goodness—You both sound wonderful—and as I said, Travis's laugh is just like Daddy's— from the belly!

I'm on my way to New Hampshire on 10 Jan 2004—probably stay 3 months—to take care of the boys—Anna drives 6 miles to Worcester Mass to the College of Pharmacology. Sometimes in inclement weather she stays down there with a friend—otherwise she is commuting every day. She's #2 in her class of 100 students—(many of them are MD's) and she loves the work, and will get her PhD in about a year and three quarters—So, I'll do anything to help out with her little family and see her through this rigorous schedule. The boys are 14 and 8 now—and they are sweet boys—I guess we all adore our grandchildren. And I was lucky. I had Sadie's 2 boys for one whole summer at ages 5 and 10—we're bonded!—and now with Anna's boys, it is the same.

Brother Bill's two daughters are: 1) in Medical School and 2) in Design School—in South Carolina and Georgia—respectively. They are 23 and 27 and are working hard at their chosen fields. Sadie's two sons are biologists—one in Oregon and the other in Sekiu Washington—And they love what they're doing—both married of course. And guess what!—we are the elders—now! Boo-hoo!!!

Thank you for the "Applets and Cotlets" a real Washington famous product! Stay warm and healthy and happy with some of your family close by.

Lots of Love from Texas!

Sarah

was similar to their father's.

LETTERS FROM TRAVIS

The next letter is more of a personal one. In the fall of 2004, Aunt Sarah writes my mother and acknowledges that my father has entered a memory care facility, which is located near Lake Forest Park. This facility was one of four that Dad entered. Also, Aunt Sarah has returned from New Hampshire to her home in Texas and

---

Sarah's Letter to Lucia – October 6, 2004

Dearest Lucia,

    I know how devastating it is for you to have had to take Travis to the memory care facility but, also how comforting it is to have your adoring and helpful children share that burden with you. You and I are so fortunate to have our wonderful children—what a blessing. I'm sure Steve is a big help around the house, but they all must be anxious for you to be relieved of that responsibility—And a house is a huge responsibility.

    I am still tackling the yard after my extended stay in New Hampshire. And now my fridge is on the blink—leaking water from I don't know where—and I can't seem to find anyone to fix it! It still works—just leaks!

    Anyway, I'm relieved that Anna no longer has to go down to Worcester, Mass to classes. She has taken her last final. Now all she has to do is intern in pharmacies—retail and hospital M,T,W,Th and Fridays 7-5. No pay—a requirement of the college.

MEMORIES AND FORGETFULNESS

So, I'm helping out there with checks and care packages—She'll be doing this until the end of March, I think. Then, she gets her degree. Whew! It has been a long tough 3 years—for her—and proud Mama, I am—She maintained an A- average—going to school Monday through Friday and working in a pharmacy Saturday and Sunday—that was for pay.

Well, so much has been going on these past many months—for all of us! I hope you are able to get some rest. And perhaps when your situation which won't require such a big house responsibility.

I'm going to make a copy of the picture the girls and I took of the house Travis and I grew up in when we drove to Hingham last year (on Main Street). The owners saw us taking the picture and after learning that I had lived there some 65 years ago, they invited us in and we spent a delightful hour or so with them. Anyway, I'll send that picture to him. I'll try to keep in touch with him via mail—I don't suppose there's a phone available.

If he's not able to read sometimes glasses get lost or misplaced, I should send the letters to you to take to him. You can let me know if that is the case.

Anyway, just let me know I'm thinking of you and the difficulty you have been going through.

Much love, my dear

Sarah

reminisces again about New England. She asks if she can contact my father by phone and wonders how to provide him with memories of Hingham.

LETTERS FROM TRAVIS

In her Christmas 2006 letter to Mother and Dad, Aunt Sarah offers a glimpse into her life.

Sarah's Letter to Mom and Dad after Christmas 2006

December 29, 2006
Dallas TX 75234-3823

Dearest Lucia and Travis—

It seems like yesterday that I visited in Seattle—The older I get the faster the days go by! It was marvelous seeing you both and part of the family. I can't believe our "kids" are all "grown up". And your sons are so admirable—with your oldest the "leader of the troop" and so handsome. How I wish we all lived closer. I have to blame WWII for sending us all over the world and then plopping us down somewhere—and for us that is where we stayed! Neither Will nor I felt we had a "hometown" so we seemed to have let the wind blow us around—No, actually, it was the Army that did it! However, travel is easy and this last trip was great. And I also applaud you both for having your pictures done almost yearly. I wish Will and I had done that. It seemed that we flew through the years, hardly stopping to take "time out"!

Anyway, I take a lot of "time out" these days. I enjoy seeing Anna and Richard and their boys, quite frequently. They are all darling to me. Richard is a most thoughtful person and a marvelous Dad to those boys—not his own, of course, but they adore him.

Anna stays busy with her job—and those three years of driving 60 miles a day to get her pharmaceutical degree was well worth it, and she is so happy that she did it. And I do think that it has encouraged Sadie to go back to school!

With all of these smart people surrounding me I feel like a dunce! Somehow I missed the boat when it came to increasing my education. Oh well…Too late now!

I don't know whether you remember that on one of my trips to New England—i.e. Massachusetts—Anna, Sadie and I drove down to Hingham. Of course, they were both interested in where "Mother" grew up. So, I showed them the house on Main Street—and we stopped to take a picture of the house. The lady who owned the house saw us and we explained that I had grown up in that house and was showing my two daughters where I had lived. The lady was delighted and showed them the inside of our old Main street house—and, of course, as I looked at the inside and the steep stairs to the 2nd floor—and how small it all looked. I couldn't believe my eyes. It looked <u>so small</u>! How we have changed! I enjoyed my trip and to be honest, was glad to live in spacious Texas! You must feel the same way in your beautiful hilltop home in Seattle—with lots of love to you and Lucia—It was so much fun seeing you both—Take good care of yourselves.

I love you both

Sarah

In May 2012, Aunt Sarah passed away from complications of dementia. Her family noticed that she was showing signs of forgetfulness in 2009. *Aunt Sarah spent the last three years of her life in Missoula, Montana with her daughter, Sadie.*

BOOK 2
FAILING MEMORY

circa 1999 Travis and Lucia

Lake Forest Park

circa 2002 Dad, Mother and me

Bend\

circa 2002 Dad Bend

circa 2007 Dad and Me

MEMORIES AND FORGETFULNESS

CHAPTER 11 – DEMENTIA -THE START (MY OBSERVATIONS)

In 1994, Carrie and I lived in eastern Oregon. On a spring weekend, we left for the Seattle area to celebrate her sibling's (one sister and two brothers who were all born in the month of April) birthdays. After being married for nearly 22 years, we could travel with less restrictions because our oldest child, Hettie, skipped off to college creating space for us and Marcella was a senior in High School. Emma was also at home. To escape from the day to day drudgery, we journeyed to Seattle because we could visit our families of origin and have free room and board. Carrie and I felt comfortable there. Our families accepted us unconditionally.

During that weekend, I visited my parents and "carried on" a conversation with my father. He described his approach to teaching and life. Previously, Dad had volunteered to tutor students at a local high school and he felt good about his ability to reach young people again. He was well liked. Dad put on his educator's hat and asked pertinent questions of the young person to guide them to the proper answer.

When I was growing up, he practiced with me, so I knew his approach. He enjoyed tapping into the minds of young people and guiding them to a final answer of a puzzle they were trying to solve. This was called the Socratic Method and he created dialog between students to draw out the conclusion. He would ask, "What do you think the answer is?" When the pupil answered, Dad responded with a question that challenged or refuted the answer. He felt the young person would learn much more and retain information if they figured it out themselves.

Tactfully, asking questions worked better than providing rote answers. When Dad used his method to teach me, I felt good about myself because in the end, I had solved a problem. Dad worked hard to perfect this technique. He never made me feel stupid and was not demeaning. His conversational approach appealed to me as he guided me to the correct answer.

Also, he suggested that writing letters kept the mind alive and talked about writing letters to Aunt Sarah. At least once per month and often weekly, he wrote his sister letters, discussing issues of the day or simply what the week had been like for him. Writing helped him keep mentally alert and in touch with people. He encouraged me to write too. Being lazy, I did not see the value of doing what he suggested. I kept myself busy with work and "life on the job," as well as raising a growing family. I preferred to talk on the phone to family members, email short notes or simply visit relatives. I think that's why I liked coming to the Seattle area. Writing seemed "old school" and time consuming. At that time, seeing family face to face appeared to be more important. I viewed myself operating in the age of computers and Dad functioned in the age of typewriters and cursive writing.

Although, I did not listen, Dad tried to explain how writing required the author to contemplate the topic and then revise it to convey the exact meaning. This brain exercise generated critical thinking by connecting the emotional with the cognitive parts of the brain. Writing took discipline and hard work to be effective. It structured the mind and helped to develop better reasoning skills.

Further, Dad would elaborate on the fact that the

reader's experience of interpreting a letter transported them into the writer's world and the experience was enhanced if the writer wrote in cursive. Although, cursive writing may be hard for some individuals to read, it reflects the personality of the writer and provides a deeper meaning of what is being conveyed. The shape of the letters, the size of the words and the idiosyncrasies of how letters are written communicate a uniqueness of the writer's thoughts and ultimately provides meaning to the reader. This uniqueness in communication conveys more than just the words themselves. When the reader interprets cursive writing, it encourages thoughtful understanding of the sentences. Writing was second nature to my father and Aunt Sarah. He loved corresponding with her.

During that trip, he voiced a concern to me "Larry, keep your mind active. Don't retire too soon. I made that mistake." He recalled the story, when as Vice Principal at Roosevelt High School, he grew tired of being the disciplinarian. He had to call parents and discuss student's poor academic performance or behavioral problems.

FAILING MEMORY

Dad excelled at his job. As a result, there were students who jeered at him in the hallway, some feared him and often parents hated him. The teachers and administrators admired him, because he worked hard to squelch or contain difficult disciplinary cases. Teachers were free to do what they do best; teach. However the roll of being a disciplinarian took a toll on him and Dad made the decision to retire early.

One day, after he decided to retire, Frank Hanson, the Franklin High School Principal, called him. Dad recounted his conversation to me, "Frank told me, Travis I want you to come back to Franklin as Vice Principal." Flattered, Dad remained committed to his retirement pledge. He told him, "I'm sorry, Frank but I'm planning on retiring at the end of this year. I've made up my mind." He continued in confidence, "I need a break. The vice principal's position at Roosevelt, while a good position, is wearing on me. The disciplinarian role is tough. I'd like to take you up on your offer, but I think it is time for me to leave the Seattle School District." Dad parenthetically told me, "And that was that." Frank responded, "Well, I can't say I'm not disappointed, but I fully understand. You need to do what is best for you." A year later, Frank retired as well.

Dad pondered, "You know I think Frank tried to tell me something that day. I think, he wanted me to go back to Franklin so when he retired I would be in a good position to become Principal at Franklin. I wish I hadn't been so hasty." He continued, "I think I could have enjoyed being Principal keeping my brain active."

***

When Dad retired, he wanted to enter the real-estate business full time. He had a partner, an educator, Johnny Walker. I thought Dad joked when he told me his name, but Mr. Walker was a real person in Dad's life. Johnny and Dad invested in properties together on several occasions and had made some money on the side. When Dad retired, he believed that he would be able to devote more time to his properties, assure the rentals stayed in good order, collect rent and sell the properties when the time looked right. He felt he could remain active.

In reality, the real estate business did not take off

like Dad had hoped. He purchased properties as far north as Rockport and as far east as Roslyn and Ronald, Washington. Financially, my Dad was "stretched thin." He did not have the cash for more investments. Johnny went on to other things and the partnership dissolved. However, Dad maintained the properties he owned. He loaned money to his children and felt good that he was able to help us from time to time.

Most of what Dad touched turned into figurative gold. As an example, when he came to Pendleton in the spring of 1994, toward the end of his real estate ventures, he talked to me about investing. Although, I remained skeptical, he said, "Larry, I think Pendleton is ripe for development. I'd like to buy some property in this booming real estate market with you and gain a return on our investment." I decided to play along. I said, "A retired guy from our church became a real estate agent in town. I think he might be able to help us." So, with enthusiasm, we left the house to talk to our agent. He showed us not one vacant lot with a nice view but four near the top of the hill. We could buy any or all the lots. I suggested that we start out small. Dad got serious and said let's take two. We purchased both lots for $10,000 total ($5000 each). Dad knew a bargain when he saw one. He said, "Larry, I'll purchase both lots and when we sell it we can split any profits." That offer, pleased me; a deal too good to be true. I invested nothing. When Dad sat down with the agent and wrote out a check, just like that, I was amazed. We felt the deal fell into our laps.

The two vacant lots were filled with grass and sagebrush that overlooked the North Hill and Reith Hill to the west. Forestry was in my blood. For more than ten years, I worked at the Timber and Lands section of a railroad company and at a local government as a Forest and Range Manager. I felt the lots needed to have at least a bush or tree on them. I obtained a handful of small pine saplings to plant on the property and talked to the neighbor about paying him a monthly sum to use some water to sprinkle the trees daily. I envisioned my own forest on these city lots, in the middle of the desert, where the only thing that grew well was wheat. My forest became a mini-project. It was located near the freeway on the south side of town at the top of a hill. The lots had good access to electricity from a nearby power pole, water, sewer and natural gas in the street. It would make a good home site for someone. I think, Dad hoped that I had intentions to build on the property. That was not in my plans. Still, I viewed it as an investment without risk. I expected someone to drive by, see the trees and think that it would be a nice place for a house.

After babying the trees for about a month, our real estate agent called me out of the blue and said, "Larry, you know those lots you just purchased? Are you interested in selling them? I have another buyer." I asked, "What is he offering?" The agent said, "Name your price." I smiled. "Let me talk to my father." I called Dad and told him about the potential sale. Dad said, "By all means. Do you think we could double our money?"

I said, "I don't know, but the agent said we could name our price." Dad replied, "Then, let's sell the lots together and offer both the lots for $22,000. That includes an additional 10% for the realtor and title fees and see what they say?" I said, "Okay then." I asked, "What if they only want one of the lots? Do we sell just one?" Dad said, "No, let's sell them both. The lots are small and they will want both lots to build something substantial anyway. We can always reconsider if they turn us down." I responded, "I'll call the agent."

I called and we received the full price we wanted for the lots. I was elated that I had received the quickest $5,000 that I ever earned without investing any money. Dad grinned too, pocketing his extra $5,000, as well as making back the money he originally invested and then some.

***

In 1997, Dad made an appointment to visit his doctor with a list of complaints. He was concerned about his impotence, high blood pressure and a host of other issues. In short, all at once, it seemed like his body was falling apart. Also, he was diagnosed with early signs of dementia.

His real estate and stock market investments had been good to him, but in 1997, he began the arduous task of consolidating his land and stock holdings.

My father knew about real estate, but the more property he owned the more his income taxes became complicated. Earlier, he hired a tax accountant to help him "square away" his books. Dad's complicated real estate and stock portfolio became difficult to manage in terms of the tax laws. He owed the IRS some money and decided to use the tax accountant on a regular basis. By 1997, he still had a good portfolio but it was pretty scattered. He began to realize his limitations. As an example, he ended up selling the Roslyn and Ronald, WA properties and began moving assets into mutual funds.

I think my dad reflected on his financial situation since he retired and was disappointed. His steady income were the pension and social security checks that he received. This income was not high enough for him to invest his money as he had done in the past. His memory began slipping and he could not readily keep track of what was needed to take place with the investments.

***

Dad always liked doing crossword puzzles. Now, because he had been diagnosed with dementia, it was important to him to show patience and perseverance when performing a task. He took up the puzzles in earnest, to keep his mind active. He liked vocabulary words and enjoyed figuring them out. Also, he, like my siblings and I, enjoyed doing jigsaw puzzles with the pieces spread out on a coffee or card table. As a family when I was a youth, we worked for hours trying to fit the puzzle piece together to create the final full picture. It provided us with a sense of a special talent, when we were able to find the small piece of the larger puzzle. My father developed a renewed interest in all these puzzles that we had and it seemed to be more important than ever to him.

***

In the spring of 1999, I returned to the Seattle area from Oregon. My father said, "Larry, why don't you take a walk with me."

I said, "Great. I'd love to."

I had no idea what he had in mind for me. We put on our hats and coats and started out the front door. Just outside of the house, rhododendrons bloomed with brilliant dark red lush flowers juxtaposed on a background of large waxy green leaves that were from the plant. I noticed the fragrance as we stepped onto the porch. The sweet smell permeated the air, but I found it difficult to tell if the rhododendron or the daffodils in the garden next to the house produced the scent. The bright yellow daffodils gave a stark contrast to the rhody's. We continued to walk down the street. Everything appeared to be in bloom. The birds sang and the old crow high in the Douglas fir cawed as we walked by the tree. He must have thought we invaded his territory. Dad theorized that the bird was hungry and hoped we would toss him a bread crumb or something when we returned.

We chit chatted and talked about springtime in Seattle. It was truly a joyous time of the year with a lot of promise ahead. We talked about the new growth and the plants that seemed to get greener with every day. But, something nagged Dad, I could tell; something significant bothered him and he wanted to get it out. I had this odd feeling, considering the discussion we just had about spring and new life. He tried to find the right words to make a transition from one topic to another but could not at that moment.

We walked down to Bothell Way, crossed at the

light as the cars stopped for the cross traffic. Dad and I found the Burke-Gilman Trail which was located across the highway along Lake Washington. We started walking along the Burke-Gilman Trail, which was paved. People were riding bikes, walking, running and exercising along its straight, narrow route. Log Boom Park became our destination which was about a mile from Lake Forest Park where we entered the trail. The heavy traffic noise from Bothell Way subsided. Again, we could hear the birds, happy sounds of joggers and bikes as they passed us. The sunlight glistened over Lake Washington as we observed watercraft that moved back and forth over the water. The only negative words out of Dad's mouth came as joggers or riders on bikes passed us on the path. They would yell out, "On your left," or ring their bells on the bikes to warn us they wanted to pass. He mocked them, by saying in a higher than normal voice, "On your left, on your left." He was somewhat annoyed that they were passing him, but then he would return to his nature of being positive.

Abruptly, he turned the conversation to his current life. He said, "I don't know why, but I stopped tutoring at the local high school. The principal encouraged me to continue, but I told her I couldn't. I guess I was lazy." I found this statement difficult to understand; I knew he wasn't lazy. Dad loved reaching into young minds and drawing out their personality and thinking abilities. He continued to be good at his method of teaching students. I queried him more about why he quit.

Dad said, "I just can't keep up the pace. I find myself not adding value to the student and his studies." I was perplexed because this did not sound like my father. Later, I realized that he tried to explain his thinking abilities had waned. He was not able to draw out the answer for the child. Maybe, he did not know the answer himself and therefore did not know how to guide the student. Whichever the reason, sadly I knew how much he loved teaching. I wondered aloud, if he just kept at it, would his own cognitive abilities improve or at the "very least" be maintained to last longer? Maybe he quit too early?

Finally, Dad said, "There is something I've wanted to tell you for some time now. I just haven't found the way or courage. I visited the doctor a while back and now it is confirmed that I have a form of Alzheimer's or dementia, the same disease your grandmother had."

I was stunned. I remember visiting my grandmother when she stayed at the nursing home in Bothell. She asked me the repetitive questions and I gave her the same answers each time. I recalled her concern about handling all those boys at Moses Brown when they returned to school. I saw the fear in her eyes as she pictured herself waiting for them and the realization that she was unable to do the things she had in the past.

When Dad told me he had also developed vascular dementia like Grandmother, I was devastated. I did not want him to suffer like Grandmother. I did not want him to restrict his activities, where he could go, what he could do and how he needed to act. He always appeared to be a superhero, or at least my superhero. Superheroes solve problems, remain the person with the answers that you need, or is the man you seek for some sort of advice. He gave me perspectives in my life that not only changed his life but began to change mine as well. *Grief set in.*

Dazed, the beautiful and bright walk with him

seemed to take a dark turn. The future lost its rose color and light vanished during this bright sunny day. I did not know what to say. I could only listen with few or no questions. It was like a bomb dropping a few steps in front of me. I felt a deep responsibility to hold on to him, keep him safe, and not only him but my family too.

Dad tried to be reassuring. He said, "I'm not worried. It is just something I will be going through and I want you to know. I am not remembering things like I once did."

Still in denial, I protested, "But, we all do not remember things and you seem to be doing well now."

He said, "No it is confirmed by the doctor, I have dementia." He reiterated, to further reassure me, he said, "I'm not worried. I'll just take it as it comes. It'll just happen."

I responded hopefully, "Medicines can cure it, right? Science has come so far." My denial scared me as much as the disease.

He said, "No, there is no cure. The tangles and plaques develop in the brain and science doesn't know why they form nor how to resolve it. When severe, the brain atrophies and the neurons and synapses don't function like they once did. They don't know you have Alzheimer's disease for sure until they do an autopsy. Some medicines seem to help you cope with the disease but they only help with some memory retention and do not prevent or delay the disease."

Afterward, I endured silence for several steps as we continued walking all the way down to Log Boom Park and I could once again hear the buses and auto traffic along the roadway above the trail. We turned around and headed back toward the direction from which we came down. It was the Burke-Gilman trail.

He reiterated, "It'll be okay. I'm prepared for what happens." But, I still wasn't sure.

CHAPTER 12 - LIVING WITH DEMENTIA

It was official. I had to recognize the fact and come to terms with the idea of my Dad having dementia. I could no longer dismiss his words when he said "Larry, I am forgetting things." Yet, he was at ease with the disease.

During the summer of 1999, I did not understand his situation. I hoped Dad would remain independent. To me, he appeared to be the same person. I did not see any outward signs of dementia. He seemed to be sharp with a good sense of humor and was able to articulate his needs, wants and desires. From my father's viewpoint, his conversations flowed, he kept his disease and his current predicament in perspective. The continuity in his life covered up any signs of his illness.

When I made comments to him about his wellbeing, I kept a positive attitude and complemented him on his abilities and the things he did on a daily basis. I might have said, "Dad, I'm amazed at how well you do those crossword puzzles," or "Dad, your letters to Aunt

Sarah are insightful and interesting," or "Dad, I want to know about your family of origin." Also, I noticed my father tried hard to be optimistic and joyful because it was generally second nature to him. However, from a realistic point of view I saw him have some memory lapses followed with elements of depression.

That summer and fall, I came to the conclusion that I had a limited amount of time to be with him. So, I decided to record the stories he told. I went to Lake Forest Park often to visit and learn from him. He could spin a yarn with the best of them. I wanted to know what he knew about our relatives. He told me stories about my grandfather, my dad's fondness of him, his art work, and working as a stockbroker through The Depression. This was despite the fact that he had an Art Degree from the prestigious Chicago Art Institute and his degree in engineering from Yale.

Grandfather lost all his money during The Depression. Additionally, Dad told me stories about the time my great grandmother required my grandmother to divorce my grandfather in the middle of that same Depression. Later they reunited in California and remarried after World War II. It seemed like the story books are made of and people really enjoy reading. I thought of it as the consummate love story.

Still, I wanted to know more about my father. I lived with this man for the first 18 years of my life, and I loved him dearly, but I still missed significant pieces of his life. As an example, he enlisted in the Army and joined the Army Air Corps during World War II. He never talked much about the war to me, my two brothers or sister when we were children. I suspect he did not want to glorify the war. However, Dad told war stories to the students at Denny Junior High School to keep their attention during class. He joked with friends about keeping the kids on the edge of their seats, but never really described any details to his own children. I did not know how he survived the many harrowing episodes he had during the war. Now, I wanted him to tell me some of those war stories. I did not know where to begin, so I began with his childhood and his father. Then, I expanded to his extended family. I compiled what I could before he could not articulate the stories anymore, but many unanswered questions remained.

MEMORIES AND FORGETFULNESS

At this time, Dad was still communicating ably, or at least he aptly covered up his inability to problem solve. Mostly he seemed alert, but some days it became difficult for him.

One day, Dad attended a meeting in downtown Seattle. I do not recall why, but it could have been a meeting about his retirement with the Seattle School District, a meeting with a lawyer over some real estate deal or to the county courthouse as well as the county office building. Here's what I pieced together based on my knowledge of the trip that he took by himself.

***

Normally, it would have been a routine trip for him, albeit a little out of the ordinary. Dad drove his small Mazda truck without incident downtown Seattle, parked it under the freeway overpass, and found his meeting without issue. He attended the meeting, took sufficient notes and started to gather his things to return home. He could think clearly in the morning and he could figure out where he needed to be and maneuver efficiently through the city maze. But, in the afternoon, he had many things on his mind and must have found it difficult to think clearly.

He reached into his pocket, found his truck keys and set off to retrieve his vehicle and head home. There was just one problem. He could not remember where he parked his little white pickup truck. After walking all over downtown Seattle, Dad remembered he parked under a bridge but he could not draw from his mind an image of where he parked, nor could he remember the bridge and direction from the meeting room he needed to go. He wandered the city for about two hours trying to envision what the area looked like and where he parked the vehicle but to no avail. Dad headed southeast down 6th Avenue looking in the parking lots under the freeway with the viaduct above. He walked to Yesler Avenue until he realized that he had gone too far. Then, he turned around and walked back through each parking lot but still could not find his truck. The more he looked the fewer things looked familiar. Finally, after looking high and low for his vehicle he gave up.

It turned dusk, became late and Dad started having trouble seeing as well as remembering. At that point, he decided he needed to find another form of transportation because dinner time was approaching. He felt that it was prudent to consider alternatives; since it was now rush hour. Dad remembered he had rode the bus and had money in his pocket. However, he just wasn't clear where and what bus to take.

Dad remembered previously, he caught express buses that took him to Lake Forest Park and when he reached the appropriate location, he could just walk up the hill from the bus stop. It seemed to be an easy fix for the night and he planned to come back in the morning and find his pickup.

Dad headed down the sidewalk to Marion Street and 2nd Avenue. He went across the street to the bus stop, purchased a ticket and hopped on a bus that said express. On that crowded bus, a nice young man stood up and gave Dad his seat. He accepted gratefully and finally relaxed. Sitting helped Dad regain strength because he had walked so far. His feet hurt and the walk had tired him out. Dad eyed the young man as he got off the bus about two stops later. The young man waved to Dad as he departed and Dad waved back settling into his seat. He hoped to be home soon.

The bus traveled through an area that was unfamiliar to Dad. On this day, what was "unfamiliar" had become the norm for him. He was not worried. Once he got closer to home, he knew he would recognize the streets and "do what he had to do." He replayed the events of the day in his mind and still wondered where he parked his vehicle. It did not matter, because for now, he was safe on the bus. As it got darker, he was glad that someone else was driving. He knew he did not drive well at night. His cataracts obscured his vision and that made everything appear to be cloudy. The bus took some twists and turns and finally got onto the freeway. Thinking that it would not be long now before, "I am home." Dad closed his eyes and tried to doze, but the noise and rumble of the glass windows on the bus kept him awake. Every once in a while, he would open his eyes and see buildings or pavement flash by. When he closed his eyes and opened them again, Dad thought that he saw an airport. He chose to ignore this sighting.

Dad may have dozed again, but this time with his eyes open, he heard the driver boom out the out the words, "Federal Way, next stop." Now, that was a shock. "Federal Way," he must have heard that wrong. Federal Way was far to the south, which was in the opposite direction he wanted to go. It could not be right. The driver made some turns and ended the ride at a bus stop. Passengers piled off. The station did not look familiar. Dad stayed on the bus. He was not sure of much of anything these days and especially the last few hours. Through the haze in his mind, he had the first real inkling that he might be in trouble. At the next stop, about half the bus emptied and very few passengers got on.

The bus driver closed the door and began to take off. A couple of turns and they were back on the freeway. Dad tried to "settle in." Again, the bus left the freeway, found a major road, and sped down it which led to another freeway. The bus crossed this road and passed the "Outlet Collection; Seattle."

The bus driver's voice boomed this time with the words, "Next Stop Auburn." Now, Dad was aware of the fact that he made a serious mistake and needed to get off the bus. This must be the southern express and he wanted to go north. He needed to find another bus that was going in the right direction. Dad was perplexed but determined that he would find his way home.

Dad knew Mother would be worried. It was likely that she had determined he met someone and wanted to go to coffee with them. Often, he befriended people and was delayed because he liked to talk, but it was uncharacteristic of him to forget the time as well as his responsibilities at home. It nagged at him. He knew Mother expected him to arrive home around 6:00 p.m. because his meeting should have ended at 3.

Dad talked to the driver and he told him the number of the next bus he needed to take that was headed north to Lake Forest Park. It was getting late. The bus driver said the last bus leaving Auburn is at 6:30 p.m. It goes to Renton, but from there it goes up the east side of Lake Washington to Bellevue and Redmond, and not to Lake Forest Park. From Renton, he needed to double-back downtown. Dad climbed aboard the last bus from Auburn to Renton per the instructions he had received from the driver. Dad realized that the directions he had been given and understood were already becoming "muddled" in his head. Since, he was less familiar with the southern part of Seattle and it was late as well as dark, he became a little anxious.

Dad struggled to solve his problem, tried to keep his wits and not panic. He knew he had to ask questions and rely on others. In the past, he was not afraid to ask questions. Dad sensed that he had to rely upon others for help because darkness had set in, he was traveling an unfamiliar route and this was necessary for him to survive. The bright lights on the buildings of the businesses they traveled passed made him squint and the neon signs "stabbed" him in the eyes at times. Trees adorned the side of the street and it was surprising how black it could be traveling though noncommercial areas. He was not sure where he was, but had been told he was headed to Renton.

From that point, he would be able to negotiate the King County Metro Bus System, but would need help from bystanders and bus drivers. He planned to ask questions until he got the answers he needed; "trusting people along the way." He listened for the bus driver to say "Next stop Renton" and immediately Dad got off the bus when it arrived at Bay One Renton Transit Center. It was nearly 7:30 in the evening. Where did he go from here?

Dad thought hard, asked experienced bus drivers questions and concluded, "I want to go back to Seattle to catch the Lake Forest Park express bus." Again, he reminded himself that was the way he knew and others had advised him to go that way as well. It was getting late and he had no idea when the buses ran and what time they stopped at night. He asked a bus driver on a smoke break what bus he should catch to downtown Seattle. The bus driver said, "Catch the Metro 101. At Jackson and 4th catch the 522." Dad wrote the numbers down on a piece of scrap paper, and thanked him. He looked for Metro 101. Through asking some additional questions, he learned he had about 20 minutes to kill and found he needed to walk to and wait at Bay 5 which was not too far away. He found a nice middle aged lady to talk to while he waited. Also, she had planned on taking a trip into Seattle. When the bus arrived they all boarded and he set off to Seattle again; back to where he had started his "bus adventure."

About 8:13 p.m., he boarded the 101. It was an

older bus, not an express like the one he had taken earlier. Dad thought, "This would do." "Just get me to downtown Seattle where I catch the correct bus that goes back to Lake Forest Park." Dad lost his self-confidence. He had relied on strangers and the directions they gave him in the hope that he would be home soon. Therefore, he concentrated on the important questions he needed to ask to help his disoriented mind. The night continued to be very dark outside the bus, but now the city lights began to comfort him. The bus seemed to stop many more times along this route than the other bus ride. Exhausted, he discovered a lack of friendly faces on the bus. Most of the people read their newspapers or books, slept or just looked outside as the city life passed by them. Really, no one spoke. Dad exchanged polite short conversations with several riders before everything returned to being silent, except for the rattle of windows and the surging transmission of the bus when it stopped or accelerated. Dad tried to close his eyes, but remained fitful and a little scared. As the bus wound downtown, it looped to the underground tunnel. He would hear names like "Next stop, International District/China Town." He was tired and did not know where to get off to catch his next bus, when he heard "Fourth and Jackson at King Street Station." The bus driver looked at Dad and said, "This is your stop. Time to get off." He took his cue and Dad prepared to leave the Metro 101. He stepped off the bus onto the platform. Knowing that he needed to change buses, Dad found his scrap of paper that said "522." Bus 522 must be the Lake Forest Park express bus. He looked at signs and asked questions about the 522 bus to people who were "passersby."

Dad found a nice man who spoke broken English, but he was not sure of the instructions he had been given, so he asked a lady. She pointed to the board that showed the 522 schedule and said, "That is the bus you want." He waited until he saw the 522 bus and it said, "Woodinville" on its reader-board. Woodinville is three towns further along the route passed Lake Forest Park. He knew she had given him proper instructions. The lady came up to Dad and said, "This is it," so he boarded the bus. The bus continued down 4th street. This bus driver boomed out, "Next stop, King County District Court, 4th and James," "Next Stop Columbia Center, Fourth and

Cherry," and finally "Westlake Park, 4th and Pike." The bus turned up Pike Street and lumbered to 8th Avenue then turned on Olive Way. As he sat on the bus, Dad recognized some of the names of the streets but still could not be certain of the pathway the bus was traveling. He started to ask questions of other passengers. Often, he would receive a strange look or a curt answer. He could not afford another mistake. It was approaching 9 p.m.

Finally, feeling a little dejected, Dad's confusion was apparent. The young lady who was sitting next to him said, "We'll be on the freeway soon. I promise. You'll be okay, and I'll let you know when we get close to Lake Forest Park." Dad was grateful for the help, and he realized that things were finally looking up. The lady had offered him some help and lent a friendly face.

The bus climbed toward the freeway. Finally, Dad saw some familiar landscape as they approached and entered the freeway that was headed north this time. He gained some self-assurance as the bus crossed over the waterway that connects Lake Washington to Union Bay. He saw the familiar University of Washington commercial area near the freeway. Then, the bus left the freeway passing by the somewhat familiar Green Lake commercial district. He thought he remembered several stops along Lake City Way, which eventually became Bothell Way at 145th Street that he knew fairly well. At least now, he saw surroundings more clearly and knew he was on the correct bus. It was not long before the bus made to Shoreline near his home. He knew he needed to get off at the next stop. Dad was elated that he remembered this familiar territory. His adrenaline surged as he thought he might find his way home in spite of being tired. As he approached, it was just a matter of time before the bus would be stopping and he would be getting off. He did not need to have the bus driver tell him. The pleasant young lady sitting next to him nudged his elbow and said, "This is your stop," as the driver said forcefully, "Next stop 170th and Bothell Way." Dad gathered what few belongings he had, looked out the window to see the local coffee shop near his home, and thanked the lady and driver profusely as he exited the bus. He could hardly wait to see his spouse.

When Dad arrived at the bus stop, it was 9:34 p.m. He knew to cross Bothell Way and hike up the hill to the house. His tiredness gave way to exhilaration. He was exhausted from his day's adventures and his blood now surged through his body at an exciting speed. It took forever for the light to change and when it did, he bounded across the highway like a 20 year old kid. Dad arrived at the first hill and finally felt his age as he continued to climb. Even with the adrenaline shooting through his bloodstream, he had to stop half way up. He began to trudge home; one foot in front of the other.

Dad crossed the street at the top of the hill. Then, he headed and then up 174th Street for the last long block near the house.

It was 9:45 p.m. when he arrived home, could not find his key and had to knock on the door.

Meanwhile, Mother had not sat idly by. She contacted my brothers. First, she called my brother, Mike, to see if by chance Dad had stopped at his house or called him for some reason. Mike had not heard from him. Then, she called Steve, and he had not heard either. Mother thought she might have to call the police.

When she heard the knock, Mother came running

to the door, opened it and gave my father a big hug. "I was so worried about you. Where have you been? I called Mike and Steve and some of the neighbors. I nearly called the police. Mike started to get ready to look for you." Dad couldn't get a word in edgewise, when Mother asked "Have you had anything to eat? Are you hungry?" Dad finally responded, "A little."

Dad was famished, but mostly exhausted and happy to be home. Through the misadventures and the excitement of being home he forgot he was hungry until he was reminded by Mother. She gave him a sandwich and she called Mike to let him know Dad was home. Meanwhile, Steve stopped by the house to support Mother, greeted Dad and gave him a big hug too.

Dad was amazed with himself. He solved his problem; he found his way home.

That night, Dad slept well and the next day all he wanted to do was rest, look out his picture window and enjoy life. Finding his vehicle did not enter his mind, nor did he think anything unusual had happened to him the night before. Grateful to be home, he did not want more misadventures and he simply put things out of his mind. Mother and Steve queried Dad later that morning as to what he remembered. Obviously, Dad had a general notion about what had happened and even a foggier notion about where he may have parked his small pickup truck. As Dad tried hard to recount his story, he thought it must be parked under a bridge downtown. Mother listened intensely. Dad's adventure home became somewhat of a mystery to him and he was puzzled why he was being asked so many questions. He just knew he was home. Mother called her friend Jean, and they went downtown to locate Dad's pickup truck in order to bring it back to Lake Forest Park.

After, searching the downtown area for some time, they did not find the vehicle parked anywhere Dad had vaguely described. Finally, they ended up contacting an impound lot, found his truck and paid the bill. Jean drove the pickup back to Lake Forest Park and Mother followed her. Once again, life became whole and everyone relaxed.

CHAPTER 13 - 50TH WEDDING ANNIVERSARY

I learned about Dad's "lost truck experience," the weekend I arrived in Seattle which followed the incident. Everyone involved expressed their shock because our father had always been alert with a command of his surroundings and had few mishaps of this nature. The dementia must have contributed to his disorientation. I think from Dad's perspective, it scared him. For the rest of us, we did not care to see this situation repeated. Therefore, whether it was right or wrong, we all became more protective of our father.

In the fall of 1999, we realized that Dad needed to feel he was independent and a functioning member of society, despite his dementia; especially in the early stages. Establishing that independence was a hard balance because it was like raising children. You do not want them to inadvertently harm themselves. We needed to learn how to weigh Dad's ability to make mistakes but at the same time keep him safe. It took more than just Mother to do this for our father.

MEMORIES AND FORGETFULNESS

Dad needed to use his mind or it would atrophy. He continued to be diligent about his mental health which included problem solving abilities. He walked and exercised on a regular basis, which kept his body fit. Also, he continued to solve crossword puzzles, read and write. Willingly, he did projects for Mother around the house. Dad wanted to continue to be optimistic and have an "upbeat life" for as long as it was possible.

***

One day, during another visit, I went to the bank with Dad. I suggested that he may want to withdraw money because the family had planned to attend an event. I thought, he should have a "few" dollars with him if he decided to buy something to eat. I wanted to give him as much latitude as I could by allowing him to make decisions which I felt would generate good mental health.

Dad agreed with me that he may need some money and decided to make a withdrawal from his account at the bank.

The employees at the bank greeted my father by his name. Everyone in the Lake Forest Park branch participated in this delightful small town custom. Since, they knew my father and mother well, I introduced myself but stayed in the background. Dad went to the counter and pulled his debit card out of his wallet and said, "Larry how much do you think I need to withdraw?" That became an opportunity that I squandered because of what happened next. "I can't help you with that Dad. You need to decide," was my reply. At the time, I was mistaken and thought I had no business telling or even suggesting what he may need. Dad said, "Okay then, $500." He gave the teller his card and withdrew $500. I did not say a word in order to protect him from being embarrassed.

When we returned home, I needed to tell my mother what happened and she knew what to do in order to correct Dad's decision. A little later Mother and Dad were alone downstairs and she asked him, "Did you withdraw some money out of the bank?" Dad said, "Yes." She asked, "How much?" He opened his wallet and showed her the $500. She suggested, "I think that's too much money but you can keep $20 for today and I'll deposit the balance back into the bank." He objected, saying, "I don't want to be humiliated when you take the money back to the bank and redeposit it in front of the bank personnel." Immediately, she understood his fear and said, "I'll take it to the Kenmore Branch not far away and no one will be the wiser." I was glad Dad relented and Mother solved my problem in an easy and succinct conversation. She saved face for father and son.

All three of us were relieved. Dad had his $20 and his dignity. I kept my self-respect and Mother worked a miracle. Now, it is true that everyday living had its challenges. As my wife says, "We do the best with the tools and knowledge we have, at the time." I have a hard time remembering that fact.

***

On Wednesday mornings, Mother and Dad joined friends from the old neighborhood for breakfast at a local Café off of Bothell Way. The friends would reminisce about the old times, when my parent's young family lived on 195th Street in Kenmore. Also, they talked about the day's events and current affairs.

One Wednesday, I went with them, and

reconnected with old neighbors. Dad relished getting out, interacting with people who knew him and he felt comfortable being himself around them. Most importantly, it gave him the opportunity to engage in light conversation. If he wanted to be silent or talk, it was okay. At the end of the meal, Bob and Harry our former neighbors and Dad rose from the table and wandered over to the counter to pay for the meal. Bob and Dad both had *dementia*. Quick witted Harry watched carefully as the two paid their portion. As they prepared to pay the bills, both Bob and Dad opened their wallets tenuously and took out twenty dollars; each to pay for the meals. Harry assured both Bob and Dad that they had received the proper change. He did this without causing a scene. Mother and Bob's wife let the men handle the cash.

Later, I asked Mother about what had transpired. She said, "It gives Dad a sense of responsibility and control over his day to day activities, which is something he rarely has now. I *salt* his wallet with cash so that he will have the proper amount to cover the payment for meals." Silently, she helped Dad without him knowing.

***

MEMORIES AND FORGETFULNESS

That fall, my brothers, sister and I cooked up the idea of having a 50th wedding anniversary celebration for Dad and Mom. It would honor them, the years they lived together and acknowledge their love for one another.

A quarter century earlier, we held their 25th anniversary celebration at my Aunt Eva's house. My mother was the second oldest of six children. There were three boys and three girls in the family. Aunt Eva was the youngest girl. At that time, she graciously hosted the event and planned to keep it as a surprise party by inviting Dad and Mother to come to her house for dinner one Sunday evening.

I remember, Aunt Eva happily arranged the intimate, joyous affair. She organized nearly everything. My sister and I sent out a few invitations to some of our parent's closest friends. Other than that, we did not have to "lift a finger" to help her. Aunt Eva asked us to be quiet about the surprise party.

As far as Mother and Dad knew, the event would be a small simple Sunday dinner. If they suspected something, we did not know it because of the expressions on their faces. The place looked festive and the guests greeted them with gracious accolades. The happy couple expressed pleasure reconnecting with friends and family. I brought my fledgling family from Oregon and met my sister, Alva, who came with Mom and Dad. Steve and Mike were both in the Army and they could not get away. Of course, my younger cousins, Aunt Eva's children were also there. Aunt Eva carried the day!

Unlike the 25th anniversary celebration, the 50th celebration could not be a surprise because we invited many more people. All my siblings, Steve, Mike, Alva and I attended with our growing families. We invited old neighbors, new neighbors, friends of our parents and of course we also invited our aunts, uncles and cousins, as well as their families. We did not expect most of the relatives to come because they did not live around the Seattle area and it would have been a long trip for them. However, Aunt Eva said, "your cousins and I will definitely come to the event, and we wouldn't have missed it for the world."

We needed a venue that would work for this celebration, and Alva had a friend who suggested a popular restaurant in the area. We chose a Saturday afternoon in January, 2000 with a no host dinner. We prepared and sent out the invitations.

My nerves got the better of me, but Dad's nerves must have been raw. I had never seen my father become self-conscious about himself as I did prior to this event. Most of the time, his self-assurance prevailed, but today was different. He fussed with his tie and coat because he wanted to leave a good impression. He was not sure about his memory, abilities or appearance. Also, I imagined that he was nervous about meeting longtime friends and whether they would notice he displayed signs of someone who suffered with dementia. I remember him asking Mother if he looked okay. Mother reassured him by saying, "Yes Travis. You look great." My mother had always been nurturing, but this time she knew why my father was self-conscious. His new behavior caused us to take notice and we all wanted to help him cope in this situation. Mother never dwelt on his concerns, but was not dismissive either. Intuitively, she began taking on more of a lead role in their relationship, guarding against being overly protective, allowing him to make mistakes and still providing support. I learned from my mother, trying to follow her lead; all the while being impressed by her abilities.

We arrived at the restaurant in separate vehicles. Dad and Mother drove their own car. My wife, Carrie, daughter, Emma, and I in another. Marcella, our middle daughter, came separately from Oregon State University. Hettie, our oldest daughter and her family came from Pullman. Carrie, Emma and I stayed at Carrie's father's house. Marcella, Hettie and Brian (Hettie's husband) stayed with my parents.

When everyone arrived, we ordered dinner, ate and enjoyed each other's company. It was a booth type setting. Although, the restaurant catered our party in a roped off section, we pretty much ate as separate family units. Emma, my daughter, took pictures to document the event. After everyone finished eating dinner, we opened up the celebration.

There were a large number of people who gathered around Mother and Dad, but some stayed in the booths where they could see what was occurring. Mother and

MEMORIES AND FORGETFULNESS

Dad opened their 50th wedding anniversary gifts.

Mother and Dad took a bite of the anniversary cake on their forks and with arms intertwined gently placed the cake in the mouth of one

another. This was a true wedding anniversary celebration. It was a joyous moment. The guests did a lot of laughing, clapping and guffawing over their experience. Family members renewed old acquaintances and new friendships were created. Generally speaking, I think the event served its purpose because it was wonderful to bring friends and family together for a pleasant time and a fun event.

Most importantly, Mother seemed pleased and made favorable comments about the evening. Dad wanted to show his gratitude too. His nervousness was put to rest. He thanked the guests for coming and his children for sponsoring the event. His gracious and thoughtful nature returned. There were no quips or jokes in his well delivered speech; just gratefulness.

MEMORIES AND FORGETFULNESS

CHAPTER 14 - MEXICAN RIVIERA

In May 2000, Carrie and I lived in Bend, Oregon. Emma, our youngest daughter, attended college in Tacoma. Our older two children either worked or began graduate studies. I worked for the State of Oregon as an Air Quality Specialist, and one Friday morning I organized a work-related meeting with people from the City of The Dalles and key organizations. This included community leaders, representatives from the fire and health departments as well as those involved with industrial sources of air pollution. We explored methods of improving air quality including ideas to limit burning in woodstoves and burn barrels on poor air quality days.

I felt good about the discussion but could not wait to get home. I anticipated a visit from Mother and Dad and expected a 3 hour drive back to Bend. I intended to return to my office, drop off my work vehicle and then leave early to return home and wait for my parents. When the meeting finished, I left about 1:00 p.m. and started driving down Highway 97 on the east side of the Cascade Mountains.

Earlier that week, I talked to Mother and Dad. I encouraged them to come to Bend for a visit. They agreed and decided to make the trip an adventure. Mother made reservations at a hotel in Redmond, Oregon which is about a 20 minute drive to Bend. She sent me her itinerary.

As I zipped out of The Dalles, the road became a blur. I drove on autopilot and started thinking about Mother and Dad's visit as well as planning upcoming events. I was worried that they would arrive at the house before me.

The road from The Dalles wound up and down hills. The Dalles is situated right on the Columbia River at 109 feet in elevation at the river and rises to about 600 feet in elevation at the southern edges of town. I began the trip back to Bend by driving through a few cherry orchards until the scenery gave way to grass and sage surroundings. Cattle roamed the grass and sage lands and it is not uncommon to see mule deer along the route.

FAILING MEMORY

The tree line of the Cascade Mountains to the west became evident looking off in the distance where a dark green patch of trees snaked around the mountains. The rugged skyline appeared as I looked to the horizon. I climbed to an elevation of 1600 feet and then the road dropped down a winding highway. This led toward the outdoor recreation town of Maupin and into the Deschutes River Valley. Maupin offers entry locations for rubber rafting or boating down the Deschutes River. Crossing a bridge to the other side of the Deschutes River, I drove up switchbacks scaling another steep hill to the plateau on top at roughly an elevation of 3000 feet. The road straightened out and I was able to see down the plateau for some distance.

As I continued driving down the straight unbending roadway, it was strange to see a small white Mazda pickup off to the side of the road; far up the roadway. I was curious and planned to stop to see if there was a problem because few vehicles travel this stretch of the road. The cars that do are driven fairly fast. I slowed down to see what problem may have occurred. It was a wonderful surprise to see my mother and dad inside the

MEMORIES AND FORGETFULNESS

Mazda. I pulled over to greet them and they responded in a happy manner, but they were also surprised to see me along this desolate stretch of roadway. They did not have any problem with their truck. They happened to be looking at a map as I approached them with the inside car light on which they turned off as I spoke. I reassured them that they were on the right road and listed the next towns they would approach—Madras, then Redmond and finally Bend. I expressed an urgency to return to the office so I could finalize my work day early and go home to greet them when they arrived.

I raced to the office and then home. An hour later Mother and Dad showed up at the house after checking into their hotel. We ate a nice dinner and talked until they went back to the hotel that evening.

Unbeknownst to me, that afternoon the Oregon Department of Transportation rerouted traffic. Dad and Mother got lost and never found their hotel. They followed the road but did not know they needed to make an additional turn. Instead of traveling toward Redmond, they drove all the way to Sisters, Oregon.

FAILING MEMORY

Late the next morning they arrived at our house. After I received them at the door, Mother and Dad told us their saga. I was mortified. Also, Dad showed me hotel registration paperwork. Dad's name was on the paper and in the place where form said "company," he had written "spouse." We laughed at the thought of the hotel manager wondering what his company produced.

Somewhere in our conversation, Dad suggested that he would like to go on a trip someplace to see the world. Mother's silence could have cut "the air with a knife." I did not recognize the situation and I pressed on with my ideas. I suggested to my parents that they sit down and talk. I volunteered to be a mediator and made suggestions about where they could go, the mode of transportation to use and I offered to go on the trip with them.

Mother did not want to go on just any trip. She needed to consider her age, medical issues and mode of transportation that would not be too stressful. The most important issue that Mother had to face was Dad's dementia. He had to be in a place where he could navigate easily without great effort. She thought hard,

189

given her misgivings about any trip. Mother knew she would be making all the decisions for both of them. Dad would just be along for the ride.

After a while, Mother suggested that we go on a cruise. She wanted to have a bathroom of her own and be on an organized trip where the activities would be planned for us. This would limit the amount of problem solving for her and Dad. I understood her dilemma somewhat and happily accepted her solution.

I talked to Carrie and she agreed to go on the trip. We planned activities that we could do with my parents and on our own. Mother thought that would be fine. At least, I would be there to help entertain Dad throughout the trip. She suggested the Mexican Rivera and I agreed, wholeheartedly.

When Dad and Mother returned home, she contacted a tour group through a travel agent in Lake City which is a few miles from Lake Forest Park. The agent set up the cruise with other retired folks from Seattle and the group took the cruise with couples from similar backgrounds. Carrie, Mother, Dad and I planned to travel on a popular cruise line in November, 2000.

The four of us took a flight to San Diego, along with the other Lake City vacationers in order to catch the cruise ship. Little did I know at the time, that we would spend much of the vacation with the same group of people, sitting at the dining table for our meals.

I was amazed that so many people had arranged to go on the same trip. When we arrived in San Diego, there was a very long line that we had to stand-in before boarding the cruise ship and checking our bags.

I was glad as we moved along slowly in line and finally completed being processed. Then, we waited on the dock for them to call our room assignments prior to us entering the ship. Again, we waited elbow to elbow. When she organized the trip, Mother selected Carrie's and my room next to theirs. She booked us cheap interior rooms. These small rooms housed a full sized bed, a dresser and a small bathroom. The cramped quarters provided us with just enough room for two people to walk past one another.

When the toilets were flushed, the waste water

went down the hole in the bowl with such gusto that a comedian during his routine in a show imitated the sound of the flushing through the microphone. This caused the audience to roar with laughter.

Entertainment on the ship included comedians as head-liners, live bands with singers, a casino and swimming pool to just name a few activities. The cruise directors organized lectures with knowledgeable experts that explained about the cultures and places we were about to visit. Also, there were numerous restaurants and eating establishments. The small cabins demanded that we walk around the ship to avoid getting cabin fever. Further, this encouraged us to explore the ship.

We set off on our adventure. The first thing that the crew required of us was to "muster on deck." Everyone was called out of their cabins. We were placed in a line around the ship as the cruise director explained safety requirements and expectations on board. When excused, Dad, Mother, Carrie and I went to the main deck to look around. We walked through the casino on the way to the outer deck and stood near the railing and waved goodbye to San Diego as we anticipated the rest of the journey. The cool breeze blew through our hair and we fortunately brought light jackets along with us.

A day into the trip, the first port of call was Ensenada, Mexico. This started our full experience of being on a cruise ship and included an understanding of the Mexican community. Since it was Sunday, Carrie wanted to witness a Catholic Mass in Mexico and Mother decided she would like to go along with her. Dad and I decided to wander through the city and experience the flavor of Mexico. Most importantly, to walk and talk like we did often, in the past. As we walked, we discussed the trip, what we saw and other topics of the day. Dad seemed to take in the surroundings, but mostly was interested in my thoughts and what I had to say.

All of a sudden, I heard my name being called. Was it a mistake? I kept on walking and talking with Dad. Then, I heard my name being called again. I looked in an open air store and saw Tony. Tony worked with me in Bend, Oregon. What was he doing in Ensenada? The same thing as I was doing; only he drove there. We stopped talking and I introduced him to my father. I talked to him for a while to compare notes. We both could not believe we had traveled half-way down the Pacific Coast and met each other in another country. I had no idea he would be there. It was an odd but a memorable coincidence.

Our visit at Ensenada ended and we went back to the ship for more experiences. The next port-of-call occurred at Cabo San Lucas. At Cabo, we took a tour of the harbor. This time Carrie, Dad, Mother and I went together. We took a small boat through the iconic Arch of Cabo San Lucas (El Archo), saw Pelican Rock and Cannery Beach. It was a sunny happy day to remember. Both Dad and Mother appeared to have a good time because we talked among ourselves comparing notes about the experience thus far and our smiles and laughter expressed our relaxed state.

We boarded the cruise ship again and sailed to Puerto Vallarta. There, Dad and Mother planned to take a tour of the city, look at sculptures like the Malecon Puerto Vallarta and other interesting sites. They seemed to enjoy their experience together. Carrie and I signed up for a horse back experience that would eventually take us up a hill overlooking the port.

FAILING MEMORY

We left the ship and boarded a bus that took us through town which included a small residential neighborhood. There was a large barn on the outskirts of the city that housed the horses we would be riding. The tour guide instructed us on the procedures for stopping the horses if we should lose or drop something. I accepted the instructions we had been given, but it seemed to me that they were overly cautious. The instructor gave me a large horse to ride because of my height, which is 6 feet tall. He told me the horse was more spirited than some of the others. Carrie was given a gentle mare to ride that would easily as well as uneventfully get her up and down the hill. The animals paced themselves as they began walking up the slope. The mare and steed we had mounted along with the other riders on their horses settled into a methodical stride. It was a nice even pace, as the animals dutifully followed their counterparts that were in front of them.

To my surprise, pleasure and in a way disappointment, the horse that I was riding, started out on the trek as a pleasant well-behaved animal. All of the horses seemed to be obedient. I grew up with horses and felt that I could handle all but the most unruly ones. We arrived at the top of the hill, dismounted and the handlers took the reins of each horse. Carrie and I went to the scenic vista to see the city and ocean beyond. We spent ample time, about 30 minutes, at the top satisfying our curiosity and romantic notions about the view.

Then, the handlers asked us to mount back up for the return ride to the station where we would catch our bus back to the ship. As before, the horses let us mount them and we started to ride down the hill. It got slightly steeper as we descended and the horses began to trot which bounced us around. They stepped lively down the hill and once we were at the bottom they began to canter. This action caused us to bounce even further.

Then, it happened! My backpack zipper unzipped and my camera sprang out. I managed to stop my horse; not quite sure what had happened. One of the handlers came up from behind and handed the undamaged camera to me. He saw it land on the ground and rode his horse to catch up with me. I was very grateful, thanked him and allowed my horse to continue the ride. I looked for Carrie and she was far ahead with the other group of riders.

FAILING MEMORY

Well, my horse decided to make up for lost time. The other horses were cantering toward the barn. I was astonished when all of a sudden I was engaged in a wild ride. He was moving fast, actually galloping toward the barn which meant our arrival time was the same as the other horses. It was a jarring experience that is completely imbedded in my brain. It has been a story to tell my grandchildren. We boarded the bus and went back to the ship for the next leg of our adventure.

We met up with my parents, swapped stories and settled into our routine onboard the ship.

As the cruise commenced, Mother decided she wanted to go see an act that was performing near the swimming pool and asked for company. I made a mistake when I said to her that I wanted to do something else and did not express an interest in going to the show. Unfortunately, Dad agreed with me and Carrie decided to do something different as well. Mother's idea of having a companion going with her vanished. Neither Dad nor I would escort her.

Mother was visibly upset and stomped off from

Dad and I. She was left to fend for herself. I felt a strong desire to talk to Mother and smooth things out with her. I made sure Dad was comfortable and went to find Mother. I found her sitting on stairs that headed up to the deck where the swimming pool was located. When, I sat down beside Mother to talk, it became obvious to me from her demeanor, that she was depressed. I expressed my regret for making the decision not to accompany her to the show. If I did accompany her, I knew Dad would have followed and this should have made her happy. My mother's mental health was worth any inconvenience on my part, so I talked to her for about an hour. She regained her composure. Since, the event she wanted to attend was over, there was no point walking around the deck once we finished talking. I felt she had accepted the situation and would be okay.

In the interim, Dad wandered the ship alone. He tried to find the cabin and kept walking around the deck, not knowing his room number. Thankfully, I found him on the same deck as our cabin. He must have walked around and around not seeing anything that was familiar to him. I felt bad, but he seemed to be in good humor about what had happened. Although, he knew something was terribly wrong, it was not until I got him into the cabin that we sat and talked. Dad listened as I explained to him why Mother was upset. Finally, Mother showed up. She and Dad reunited, without a major incident.

I went up to the upper deck where Carrie said she would be and found her listening to a band that kept playing the same song over and over again. I think it was the only one that they knew. Carrie walked away from the performance and to this day she detests that song. It is hard for me to "stomach" that tune as well.

On the cruise, we often dressed for dinner. Whether we were attending an informal or formal meal, Dad, Mother, Carrie and I always got ready for dinner as if it was a special occasion. The service for the formal dinners took a little longer. We had the same head waiter and he always provided us with a good time as we either waited for dinner or he offered his opinion on what meal to select. The waiter was from Singapore and the assistant waiter was from Ghana.

During one meal, Dad sat next to a fellow from

MEMORIES AND FORGETFULNESS

Lake City. Both men were veterans and had a great deal in common. They talked for the hour nonstop, comparing notes on WWII, military service, places in Lake City, Seattle, the Lake Forest Park government matters and many other topics. I was impressed because I knew Dad struggled to remember some things and had a difficult time during the conversation. However, he was his old self and carried on throughout the evening like a trooper. After the meal, he commented about how much he missed a good conversation and how good it felt to express himself as he did aptly, prior to the dementia. I reflected on the time that I had spent with my father and felt I needed to give him other opportunities to express himself in a similar way in other settings. Unfortunately, those moments were now few and far between.

When we arrived in Acapulco, the temperature rose to over 80 degrees and we enjoyed our stay on this warm day that in more northern climates would be rather chilly. This was a refreshing change from the cold weather we usually experienced. As a result, we saw the city in all its glory by walking or catching a cab from one end of the city to the other. The cabs seemed to be small

FAILING MEMORY

German-made cars.

So, Mother and Dad took a formal bus tour while Carrie and I took a cab going in a different direction. Mother and Dad wanted to see The Ecumenical Chapel of Peace and other sites identified on their tour. Carrie and I asked the cab driver to take us all over Acapulco and show us the sites. The driver was knowledgeable and spoke great English. He explained to us that he had stayed in the Midwest for a while and returned to Acapulco to work "with the tourist crowd." He drove us by the Ecumenical Chapel of Peace as well as other highlights of the city.

Finally, he drove us to the famed La Quebrada Cliffs. We saw brave men and sometimes women divers climb high onto the cliffs and then they took a plunge into the warm clear water below. One wondered, if they were able to make the perfect dive every time because of the narrow inlet they dived into. One false move may have spelled tragedy. But, the experienced divers attracted tourists from all over the world to watch. Carrie and I were enthralled and we stayed quite a while. Meanwhile, Dad and Mother's tour was over and we ended up in the same location. What a wonderful coincidence to cap off our Acapulco adventure. Also, one of the young divers impressed Mother so much, that she kept talking about him, and described how kind and courteous he was to her. This is because when he emerged from his dive and was out of the water he walked passed my mother. He smiled at her and offered a friendly greeting. I think she was smitten. Carrie and I laughed at the thought.

All four of us boarded the cruise ship again for a long ride back up the Rivera. The cruise-line staff had planned one last port-of-call, but it had to be cancelled because one of the ship's engines cut out and they could not fix it until we docked in San Diego. The cruise officials offered us some amenities, but they were small and did not really satisfy the passengers. Generally speaking, it was a successful and enjoyable trip. However, Mom, Dad, Carrie and I looked forward to returning to the U.S. We arrived in San Diego, disembarked and were happy except for our trying experience just prior to arriving in Acapulco, where Mother missed her program.

FAILING MEMORY

Dad appeared to have managed his dementia reasonably well at this point, but we needed to be with him at all times.

MEMORIES AND FORGETFULNESS

CHAPTER 15 – ADULT DAY CENTER

It must have been in the early spring of 2001, when I came to Lake Forest Park for a weekend as I often did, during this period of time. I drove from Bend, Oregon. It was a long five hour haul and I called Mother as we passed Issaquah which was located at the base of Snoqualmie Pass. I told her I planned to drop Carrie off at my brother-in-law's house and then I would be on my way north. I planned to call Mother again when I left Renton.

As I dropped Carrie off, my anxiety kicked in because I intuitively felt something was wrong. We arrived at Carrie's brother's house in Renton, sat in his living room briefly, and had a polite conversation with Pete and Joan, Carrie's brother and sister-in-law. Then, I explained, I needed to leave for Lake Forest Park and bid them a fond adieu.

I am not sure why I became anxious to leave. Somehow I felt an urgency to make the most of my time with Dad in Lake Forest Park. At the time, I knew Dad was not problem solving well and often forgot many important things. Besides, I wanted to gain as much insight into his background as I could before he completely lost his ability to recall information.

After I called Mother, letting her know my ETA, I left Renton and began my trek up I-405 to Lake Forest Park which was about 30 minutes from where I was driving. Several moments before I called Mother, she must have suggested to Dad, "Go downstairs and make Larry's bed, so he has a comfortable place to stay when he arrives."

So, I traveled quickly to Lake Forest Park to begin my weekend with my parents. The highway was teaming with vehicles, but the trip to Bothell remained rather fast at freeway speed. I turned and traveled through Bothell; heading on to Lake Forest Park.

After leaving the city of Bothell and nearing Lake Forest Park city limits, I came around a large bend in the narrow roadway known to locals as "dead man's" corner. I saw a man walking briskly along the highway. I looked closer and thought it may be my father. Initially, I did not believe it was him and thought I must have been mistaken.

I surmised that this must have been a stranded motorist or someone who lived nearby because of the clothes he was wearing. He did not look like he was dressed for a walk in this cold weather "let alone" a brisk hike. The man had on a plaid sleeveless sweater, khaki pants and dress shoes. As I drove by, I thought, "I'll never forgive myself, nor will Mother, if I keep driving and the man that I passed really is my father." Further, I reasoned that if he was Dad, and reached Bothell, there was no way I could find him, because I would not know which direction he may decide to take as he continued to walk. I knew there was a possibility that Dad might not stop or turn around until he became confused. It was imperative for me to find answers to the questions that were "racing" in my head. So, I turned my car around and went back to check.

I took the next left and essentially made a U-turn to get back to where I had seen the man. I saw him again and became convinced that it was Dad. I turned into a fruit stand that was on the other side of dead-man's corner and pulled a quick K turn to head back toward him as he walked toward me. Because the roadway was narrow, I pulled over into a driveway that went up a hill, stopped the car, got out and walked toward him.

When I was close enough to him, I said, "Dad, what are you doing on this highway?" He appeared to be in a very happy and jovial mood. Endorphins must have been surging through his body from all the brisk walking.

He stopped and looked at me incredulously, and replied, "Why coming to meet you, of course."

I said, "Well, am I glad to see you." I wondered if he would have walked to Oregon to see me.

He smiled and replied, "I am glad to see you too." He knew his hike was over and his mission fulfilled.

We walked back to the car, and I said, "I bet there is someone who is wondering where you are." I whipped my cell phone out from my pocket and said, "Do you want to talk to her?"

He responded with the marvel of wonder like a small child seeing an object for the first time, "On that?"

pointing to the cell phone.

I said, "Yes" and I dialed Mother. When Mom answered, I said, "I think someone wants to talk to you." As I handed him the device, Dad did not miss a beat and talked to her just like he was in the house safe and sound. Dad gave me back the phone and I explained that I had found Dad wondering down Bothell Way and I was bringing him home. Mother had no idea that Dad had left the house. I was grateful that I stopped and we could be reunited again.

Afterwards, I pieced things together. I figured out that Dad must have walked down the stairs at the house and left by using the backdoor. He headed off from the house, walking toward Bothell to find me. That meant he had traveled about 4 miles (about an hour and 20 minute walk) on foot.

***

Generally, Mother kept up her spirits but the responsibility of caring for Dad on an ongoing basis weighed on her, heavily. She placed Dad in adult day care program which was part of a local senior suite of programs for patients with dementia to relieve caregivers who needed a respite during the day. Intuitively, Dad knew that Mother needed relief. Joyfully and honorably, he agreed to go to the day care program for several hours to give "Mother a break."

Another senior program provided a basic transportation need within the Lake Forest Park and Bothell communities. When called upon with a 24 hour notice, a wheelchair access mini-bus would stop in front of the house, pick up a client, transport them to medical appointments, shopping trips, the adult day center and other locations. Mother worked with the local senior programs and knew about those services.

Consequently, Dad smiled at the driver as he walked up the steps to the waiting doors of the mini-bus which took him to the day center. He told me they drove him all over creation in order to pick up others and deliver them to their destination.

One day, while I was visiting Dad and Mother, she suggested that I should go to the day center and get Dad. Mother told me she would call and cancel his appointment with the mini-van that was scheduled to bring him home. She suggested that I stay for about an hour with Dad, see what took place and I could bring him home. Gladly, I drove to the center.

I am not sure what I expected, but I did not anticipate participating in anything; just observing. When I arrived, Dad was overjoyed and happily welcomed me. We sat in a circle and sang songs. These were songs Dad knew well and he did not need to look at the words. I on the other hand, kept my copy of the music and hoped I would not stand out as I tried to sing along. Dad and I played games with the other seniors. These were simple almost childlike games, such as bouncing a large ball to one another in a circle and the hokey pokey that would challenge their dexterity and mental capabilities.

I must express a feeling of pride for my father for his ability to see the day care center as a place where it was necessary for him to be at that time. I believe he learned how to cope with his disease and remain calm through difficult situations. Whether it was intuitive or not, Dad knew whatever help the day center provided was important for his well-being. Simply speaking, when he was at the center Mother had a break from caring for him.

Dad and the other men joked that they were inmates at the day center. They felt confined to perform activities that were often stilted and juvenile. Their daily routine may have turned into moments filled with expressions of sadness or even bitterness that normally did not last too long.

Whatever Dad and these men thought, they were determined to make the best of their situation. They complied with the requirements of making the journey from the house to the adult center and back safely again without disruption.

Dad kept a notebook and a memory journal. I never saw him write anything in his notebook while I was there. Yet, he kept his notebook handy just in case it was needed. Often, he wrote notes at home to remind himself of things he wanted to remember

My father became a new type of man and I decided I needed to view him as he is now and not as he had been in the past. Although, I was left with the void of knowing

I would never see the "old form" of Dad again. I focused on moving forward in a new direction.

When we returned home from the day center, Dad and I continued to talk and I helped him where I could around the house. Mother remained in bed during the early afternoon, trying to get some rest. I did not think much about it, but Dad off-handedly stated, "She seems to be in bed a lot nowadays." His words surprised and impacted me. I began to realize that her normal disposition had changed and was likely due to the strain of being Dad's caregiver.

Finally, Mother awoke and said to Dad, "Travis why don't you take Larry out to the garage and help him clean it up?" I was a little startled and I started to question her by asking what exactly she wanted done in the garage. Dad said, "That's okay, I know what to do." Evidently, she had made similar statements to him several times.

So, Dad and I dutifully went to the garage to clean as well as sort items. Initially, taking my father's lead, I started putting things into buckets and containers. As we talked, Dad agreed that some of the things he would never use again. Those items could go to a second hand store or other charities. We enjoyed talking and being in each other's company with a purpose of getting the garage cleaned. We spent a couple of hours at the task and I felt a sense of accomplishment afterwards.

Later that year, caring for Dad became enough of a stress for Mother that she needed not only daytime relief but also longer terms of respite. She contacted the Veteran's Administration and decided to place Dad in the veteran's home for those with dementia near Fort Lewis in Tacoma. She discussed with Dad what she wanted to do and he agreed with her. My father enjoyed getting out and meeting new people. He knew deep down inside that Mother must have some time away from him.

The Veteran's Affairs Medical Center near Tacoma offered Dad accommodations for up to a two week stay. I found out about his stay at the Center from my brother. While I was sure about the good quality of care Dad would receive, I wished mom had discussed it with me.

FAILING MEMORY

The State of Oregon provided me with generous benefits working as an Enviromental Specialist with plenty of sick leave and vacation time. I decided that I could take some time to be a caregiver for my father. Therefore, after he was discharged from the VA Center, I proposed an alternative method of taking care of Dad to Mother. Periodically, I would take Dad for a week or two to give him the care that he needed and Mother a rest. *This proved to be one of the most rewarding experiences I had with my father.*

MEMORIES AND FORGETFULNESS

CHAPTER 16 – VISITS TO BEND AND THE DALLES

Dad seemed happy to comply with the arrangement that Mother and I made about his visits with me. I would leave for Seattle, pick him up and bring my father to Bend, Oregon on a regular basis. This occurred about once every three to six months. Often, I would travel to Lake Forest Park on the weekend, pick up Dad and take him back the next weekend or the following one. It depended on the length of his stay.

Hettie, my daughter, and Brian, my son-in-law, moved to Eureka, California. Hettie, Carrie and I discussed taking a trip to Cave Junction to look at the Oregon Caves. We were trying to find a place in-between Bend and Eureka to visit as well as enjoy each other's company. Dad happened to be with us that week and the three of us packed for the trip to meet Hettie, Brian and a friend in Grants Pass, Oregon. In Grants Pass, we stayed at a hotel with 3 rooms. Hettie and Brian's friend agreed to have Dad stay with him. At the last minute, Carrie felt uncomfortable with the arrangement because she expected Dad to be disoriented, not knowing his roommate and potentially react poorly. Wisely, Carrie said, "What if your father has a concern and needs comfort?" I said, "We would be right down the hall." That did not satisfy her. She said, "I would feel more comfortable if he stayed with us." So, Dad slept in the bed on one side of the room and we felt comfortable being in the bed a few feet from him.

We fell asleep quickly. When I woke about 2 a.m. Dad was looking out the window with a puzzled look on his face. I said "Dad, you look perplexed."

He said, "I am—where am I?"

In a reassuring voice I said, "We are in Grants Pass at a hotel and are planning on going to the Oregon Caves tomorrow." He said, "Oh, Okay" and went back to bed. It bothered me that he did not remember the discussion we had planning our itinerary the day before this incident occurred. I was beginning to see a pattern. I remembered Grandmother's fears. I did not want Dad to wake a few minutes later and repeat the scenario, so I stayed awake the rest of the night. If it was necessary, I could quickly reassure him again. He never woke until morning.

The next morning when we awoke, everyone was refreshed except for me. I needed a cup of coffee. We found Hettie, Brian and their friend already at breakfast. Dad and I wandered in and I helped Dad obtain his breakfast at the buffet the hotel offered. Dad joined in on the morning conversation, asking how we all slept. He never mentioned his night's sleep. Without his prompting, again I gently reminded him of the day's itinerary and he became eager to see the Oregon Caves. We all piled into our cars and in a little over an hour we arrived at the Oregon Caves National Monument. We signed up for a tour and at the appropriate time were escorted through the entrance. Dad and I picked up the rear of our party. I made sure Dad ducked as he approached a short entryway. He took things in stride and walked carefully as we marveled at the stalagmites and stalactites throughout the cave.

The uneventful, but memorable event, allowed Dad's reactions to be appropriate all the way through the experience. Adeptly, he hid any memory loss or problem solving difficulties. I allowed him to use me as a crutch, ask his questions and be quiet when he felt the need not to say anything. Dad enjoyed talking immensely to Hettie and Brian's friend from Eureka, but never really got into great depth with his conversation. Brian's friend commented to me that he did not see signs of dementia and felt that Dad was a regular guy. By this time, Dad was proficient at covering up any of his misgivings and was able to operate on autopilot during conversations. He relied on past memories and would recall them when it was necessary. He had an exceptionally good day.

Carrie and Hettie commented to one another that Dad appeared very happy and interested in the caves. He smiled, talked, asked questions and seemed to thoroughly enjoy himself. Hettie and Carrie lamented the fact that most likely he would not remember the experience tomorrow, but for now his emotional responses remained high and no one regretted bringing him along.

That afternoon, we parted from Hettie, Brian and friend. Happily Dad, Carrie and I drove back to Bend late that evening.

FAILING MEMORY

Later that week, Dad and I discovered the Bend Lava Caves. We walked through from one end to another and then walked the trails on top of the lava beds near the caves. Dad appeared to enjoy his experience with nature but persisted being less talkative than he had been days before our time together. I was not exactly sure what to think, even after asking him, "Dad, what are you thinking about?" Also, we walked through Sun River, which is a small tourist community near Bend. Dad became a little more talkative as we drove through the community that was constructed of streets with endless round-a-bouts at every block. We were headed home.

***

I enjoyed cooking for Dad. In the morning I would wake, go downstairs, start fixing oatmeal, or eggs and bacon and on occasion pancakes. When Dad awoke, he dressed himself and came down the short flight of stairs to the dining area. It never failed; he would ask his first question of the day, "How did you sleep last night?" I answered him and then I asked him about yesterday's events. Often, he did not recall the events. Surprised, I would conduct additional query. He would ask the same questions he asked the day before and I would give him similar answers to his questions each time. This bothered me, because my encounters with Dad reminded me of a popular movie. Every day's events repeated the previous day with minor variations. Although, I tried to vary his activities, it did not seem to matter. The conversation always began the same and I provided similar responses.

***

I knew we needed to spice things up a little. He loved playing golf. I did not care how I entertained my father, as long as we were together and cheerfully he enjoyed himself. I knew of a golf course with long fairways, a few water hazards and fewer golfers on the weekdays. I drove us to Prineville, which is about 30 miles from our home in Bend. The short trip took us through some pretty juniper country. One Prineville council member described the golf course to me as a disguised sewage treatment plant.

Previously, the City of Prineville violated waste water regulations with effluent discharging or the outflowing of contaminated water into the Crooked River from the city's sewage treatment plant. To remedy the violations, Prineville elected to create water hazards with the effluent discharge into ponds at the golf course. The ponds polished the effluent by any remaining bacteria eating residual sewage before the effluent entered the groundwater and eventually reentered the Crooked River. Additionally, microbial action in the soil purifies the effluent. The effluent also helped irrigate the golf course, keeping the grass green without fertilizer. The innovative fix allowed Prineville to solve a problem and even allowed the city to earn a modest income from tourists looking for a golfing experience.

As I explained how the golf course worked to Dad, his interest peaked, but obviously he really anticipated the golfing encounter. To begin, we arrived at the clubhouse, talked to the city employee and rented golf clubs. A smile returned to my father's face. He developed a banter about golf, golfing friends, family, past and present relatives.

Dad had cataracts in both eyes which caused him to have a cloudy visual experience. He wore glasses, but they hung around his neck with a retainer strap. It did not matter that he never looked through his glasses, as he enjoyed himself playing golf. He would ask me, "Larry can you point to the pin? Show me where it is." Dutifully, I would point, he would look down my arm at the pin, take his stance and hit the ball. Invariably, it would go straight and surprisingly toward the pin. I would take my swing and sometimes the ball went straight but more often than not, I would slice it to the left or right. Therefore, the ball would go into the rough. I racked up points. Dad kept his to a minimum. We would laugh and talk about the shots. I did not care that my points mounted up twice as high on the score card as Dad's. I would not have traded these moments for anything in my life. More than playing golf, I enjoyed being with my father.

In a way, my father became a new form of himself, but at the same time he was the same person. I reacted and interacted with him much differently than I had a few years earlier. He depended on me. Still, he became my friend and partner. I took the time and "smelled the roses" to experience my father like I had never experienced him before!

FAILING MEMORY

***

On one of Dad's visits, I decided to help Hettie by driving her over packed car from mid-southern Oregon to Bend. My son-in-law, Brian found a new job at a University in eastern Washington and went there to start working. He left his job at a mill in Eureka, CA. Brian rented a large truck to move most of their belongings and Hettie stayed behind in Eureka to finish packing any remaining items. This included packing her car so she could barely see out the back. She planned to stop, leave much of the "stuff" from her car at our house, and return to Bend to collect her belongings at a later date.

Game for something new, Dad agreed to go with me to rescue Hettie's over packed car. Hettie was determined to make "great" time in her travel to meet us. Therefore, we kept in touch by cell phone.

On the way, I suggested to Dad that he drive. Dad declined, stating he did not feel confident in his abilities to drive anymore. Content, he accepted riding in the passenger seat and going along with me.

We met Hettie at the entrance to Crater Lake; she

was dog-tired. Hettie agreed to drive my car and I would drive hers the rest of the way to Bend. Dad agreed to keep her company. I hoped that he and she would develop an enriched grandfather to granddaughter rapport on the way. While they did, the trip to Bend for me went quickly and terminated with me being fatigued from the long drive. Hettie flopped on the bed exhausted when she arrived in Bend.

***

During that visit and future visits, I noticed Dad continued not to remember activities that happened the previous day. It scared me a little, because I hoped he would have stories to tell Mother when he returned from his visit to our home. I continued to develop daily activities with fun-filled things to do, in order to keep Dad's mind active. I began to realize that often he would just follow instructions and do what others thought he should do.

On other trips, when Dad came to Bend, in order to give Mother a respite from caring for him, I took him golfing again. Also, we explored quite a few places that included Santiam Pass, Paulina Peak, Paulina Lake, East Lake, the Newberry Crater and Big Obsidian Flow. We took the elevated Cascades Highway and our canoe out on Sparks and Elk Lakes.

One weekend, Emma came home from college. We decided to go to Sparks Lake and take the canoe. The lake exhibited low water that summer and we carefully maneuvered our canoe out through the boulders onto the lake proper. Dad sat on a pad in the middle with a paddle with Emma up front and me in the back. Dad insisted on paddling, but I wanted to steer the boat. Emma was an experienced rower. She learned this skill when she attended church summer camps.

I dropped Emma off on a far shore with Dad and she entertained him while I rowed back to the car to pick up Carrie. It was not very efficient, but I sat in the back as I always did trying to steer and paddle. Instead of rowing from the middle of the canoe to balance my weight, the front end of the boat went up in the air and I had little control. It remained a wonder that I did not capsize the boat. Still I persevered; finally made it back to the far shore where Emma and Dad were waiting.

MEMORIES AND FORGETFULNESS

When we arrived, I apologized for taking so long, but Dad as always with good humor said, "That's alright, Emma and I talked about the price of tea in China and we figured things out." Carrie and Emma decided to hike back on the trail. Dad, Carrie and Emma did not know that I was still mortified from my experience.

Dad and I piled into the canoe and paddled back to the starting point. Dad was sitting in the front of the boat and he became very uncomfortable. I pulled over to the shore where I knew there was another trail back to the car. Dad got out of the boat, while I paddled back to the beginning of our trip. I had much better experiences with my father in Bend than that day on Sparks Lake. When we arrived home he expressed he was happy to be back and out of the canoe.

When it came time to take Dad back to Seattle, we decided it would be a good experience for him to take the train from Portland to Seattle. I made arrangements for Mother to pick up Dad at the King Street Train Station in Seattle. Mother agreed and we drove Dad to Portland to catch the train. I did not think much about it until we got to the train station. I planned to purchase the tickets for him and the ticketing official asked for his ID. Of course, I had my identification but they wanted Dad's as he was the traveler. Without realizing it, I had left his wallet on the dresser in our house. The ticket agent took it upon himself to lambast Dad for not having his ID. I tried to explain that it was my fault, but that did not matter. The ticket master wanted to get something off of his chest. He stated, "Do you remember a thing called 9-11 (of course Dad did not), and we need to know all of our passengers. Without identification we cannot tell who is who. You could be a terrorist for all we know."

My imagination escalated, thinking of Dad as a terrorist. It seemed ridiculous to consider him a terrorist or someone who could plot anything. Obviously, he was a threat to no one.

Dad stood there, not saying a word and accepted the humiliating rebuff from this man. Finally, I had enough. Abruptly, I told the agent we would not be using the train. Instead, we would be driving Dad to Seattle and there was no need for his services. I told Dad not to worry. I would get him home safely. I called Mother letting her know the change in plans.

MEMORIES AND FORGETFULNESS

I was concerned about the obvious. First, the ticket agent had no reason to admonish Dad the way he did. Second, I became increasingly concerned about Dad's safety boarding the train by himself. How would others on the train treat Dad? Would he be treated courteously, ignored or worse, be further humiliated? I was not going to find out. We left by car for Seattle.

***

In December 2002, we moved to The Dalles which is north of Bend to be closer to Mother and Dad. I continued to bring Dad to our home and explore the area. I drove him to The Dalles, telling him we were driving down the east side of the Cascade Mountains. As a curiosity, when we got to the Columbia River I asked him which direction he thought we should take in order to go along the river. He said, "Take a right when you cross the river." His uncanny sense of direction thrilled me. I do not know if he just guessed or if he truly knew to turn right and go west. If we were to travel to Pendleton, what would he have said? Would he say. "Left to the east?" I'll never know. We turned right and travelled the short 20 miles to The Dalles. I drove up to our new home and we walked inside.

While sitting in the living room, Dad and I began chatting. I asked him what he thought of the house. He said the living room looked "commodious." I did not know what the word meant. Here's a guy theoretically suffering from dementia and he spit out the word commodious like a Rhodes Scholar. After WWII he did attend Oxford[1] for a short while but I do not think that is where the word came from. I think in the recesses of his mind he used the word and it fit. I asked him what the word meant. He said "large, roomy and comfortable." Yep, the room looked large. We placed our furniture in a way that conversation could easily take place and at the same time you could look out through a sliding glass door with picture windows, peering over the deck and beyond to the Columbia River. A commodious room fit nicely the description of the space.

That evening, Carrie and I gave Dad our bedroom so he could be comfortable and we took the bedroom across the hall. Our dog, Nala, quietly went about her

---

[1] While in the Army Air Corps, he was assigned to attend Oxford while he was stationed in England for additional pilot training.

business in the house and mostly stayed out of the way or out of sight. Late that night, Dad woke up. I thought it might be a repeat of the Grants Pass experience where he did not know where he was. As he walked by our room, I asked him, "Dad can I help you? Is there something you need?"

He responded very agitated and said, "No, I can't find what I'm looking for."

I asked him, "What are you looking for?"

In a loud voice he said, "I don't know. I can't find it."

Carrie said, "You're scaring the dog." Meanwhile, Nala had scooted down deep under the bed to hide.

Dad said, "I don't want a dog here. You need to get rid of the dog."

Carrie said, "Do you see a dog? The dog is gone."

I said, "Dad why don't you go back to bed. We'll find whatever you are looking for in the morning."

Finally, Dad calmed down. He remained agitated, but could not argue. He did not have the strength. I said,

"Your bed is in here and if you want to look at the river you can look out this window." I pointed to the narrow window at the top of the room and showed him the panoramic view of the river. Dad stood looking out the window. Most likely, he did not remember the commodious living room or where he was; scaring him further. Somehow, we got Dad back to bed and he awoke the next morning his cheery self, yet he was still contemplative.

When I considered this experience, I was too tired to think clearly when I talked with Dad that night. Whenever Dad and I talked, I tried different forms and methods of reasoning with him but this time his agitation got worse.

Oddly, Dad loved dogs. As a kid, he owned many dogs and his parents had dogs until they passed away. It was not until late in his life that he and Mother owned cats and no dogs. Perhaps, he did not remember owning the animals. Later in life his intolerance of dogs became a symptom of his dementia.

The day we got ready to leave to take Dad back

home to Seattle, he and I shuffled around doing menial tasks and tried to fill the time before we departed. A little while later, Carrie had a problem with the computer and needed my help. All of a sudden, I heard the front door close. Dad had walked out. We lived at the top of a hill on a dead end street with only one way to go which was down the hill and to the left. Any other way he walked would have led him to a dead end road, the hospital or back to our house. I helped Carrie with the computer and finally said, "Dad walked out of the house. I need to go find him." She agreed and let me go while she finished her work.

I ran down the hill until I could see him walking toward the bottom where he would either turn left or right. I called after him. He kept walking. I caught up with him and talked in a convincing manner so that he would go back to the house. He did so reluctantly, but complied. Finally, it was time for us to go and Dad's cheerful disposition returned. We left for Seattle.

***

In the spring of 2003, Emma graduated from the

FAILING MEMORY

University of Puget Sound (UPS) in Tacoma. We left for Emma's graduation. Carrie and I left The Dalles for Tacoma and my brother Steve, Mother and Dad came down to Tacoma from Seattle for the event. Carrie's Mother and her husband, and her father, Richard, also came to the graduation. Carrie's Dad's spouse had passed the previous summer. Emma's fiancé, Jason, also attended with his parents. Jason met Emma at UPS and he had graduated from the school a year earlier and left for Mesa, Arizona to start a career. He and Emma planned to live there after she graduated. He returned for Emma's graduation.

The graduation was held in the University's stadium. The extended family wore heavy coats and snuggled together in the bleachers as we squinted to see the graduating seniors. Emma walked up, collected her diploma and we could barely make out where she was as she crossed the stage. Afterward, we took pictures and joined in on the merriment at the University. Dad was sociable as he joined in the photo opportunities by standing next to the graduate.

A couple of weeks later, Jason and Emma planned

their wedding in Tacoma. Dad, Mother and Steve again returned to Tacoma for the nuptials. Just prior to the actual ceremony, our son-in-law, Brian, escorted Mother down the aisle with Dad walking fairly close behind. I could tell, Dad's confidence waned as he shuffled behind Brian and Mother. Dad sat with the other extended family guests near the front as Reverend Anthony Phinney, performed the wedding ceremony. Quiet and unassuming, Dad took in the celebration and even danced with Mother in a sweet fashionable way as their humanity, on the dance floor, swayed to the music.

The following day, Emma and Jason left for Mesa, Arizona with Jason's parents driving a trailer load of Emma's belongings. They were traveling south and stopped briefly by The Dalles to gather a few additional possessions she had stored at our house.

***

On another summer visit to The Dalles, Mother decided to come and pick Dad up. She spent an evening at The Dalles enjoying time with us. On the way back, Dad, Mother and I stopped along the Columbia River to watch the wind surfers as they went back and forth across the river. We felt like recreationers sitting amongst those folks who were sunning themselves on the beach alongside their boards. It was a pleasant afternoon. We bid goodbye at the surfer site. Mother and Dad left for Lake Forest Park and I drove to The Dalles.

MEMORIES AND FORGETFULNESS

CHAPTER 17 – MEMORY CARE FACILITIES

As the primary care giver for Dad, Mother needed to make decisions for his wellbeing, listen to him and accommodate his desires. This was a tall order for which she had no formal training. However, instinctively she knew what Dad wanted and in her quiet way went about addressing his concerns. It was paramount for Mother to consider Dad's medical welfare and safety because at this point in time she could not continue to be his care giver. Dad's daily needs were too overwhelming for her to handle.

In September 2004, Mother made the decision to place Dad in a memory care facility. She chose a facility that was located near Lake Forest Park. This place was a relatively modern, pleasant, brightly lighted residence that was under new management. The building was outfitted with staff that were trained to care for Alzheimer's patients.

A small lobby outside the locked unit allowed families to greet the staff and be sign-in. To enter, we were buzzed through a solid door that entered an area that reminded me of the outdoors (only it was fully enclosed indoors). Along a pathway, there were murals of trees, birds and other outdoor settings painted on the walls. A large mural covered the door we had just entered which led back to the lobby. I had to look carefully to see the latch and buzzer that would allow me or others out. As I looked forward, to one corner of the pathway, a rustic porch was constructed with a wooden bench swing. Continuing down the pathway, I walked around a patient lounge that resembled a courtyard.

At the far end of the walkway, I observed a dining room, kitchen and recreation gathering area for the residents. On the outside of the initial building were constructed two dorm-style wings spreading out in both directions. Walking down the hallway in the dorm-style wings, the resident quarters and bathrooms were located on either side of the wing.

Dad's cozy room was located in the first wing. His room held a single bed, night stand, a chair and clothes closet. The stark setting held the essentials that provided Dad with his basic needs.

FAILING MEMORY

When I visited Dad, I noticed he had placed his comb and notebook on the night stand. He could watch TV on a small set that was located on his dresser and his clothes were placed neatly in the small closet. I am sure all of his possessions could have been placed in a large box for the move into the facility. Dad must have felt that he had reverted to his time in the military because he was currently living in crisp new surroundings. I surmised, that unlike military personnel, the staff at the residence made him feel comfortable and relaxed.

As we sat on Dad's bed talking, a neighbor from two doors down came to visit us. The visitor introduced himself and Dad made polite conversation with him. Our guest picked up Dad's comb and began combing his hair. Dad did not notice and continued to talk to the man. He responded naturally, as if the man had brought his own comb with him. When the man left, he slipped Dad's comb into his pocket and left the room. I thought of telling a staff member about it but figured Dad may go to the man's room and use his comb there, so I did not bother. Dad did not care.

The day I arrived at this memory care facility, Dad

showed me around. He liked to walk around the courtyard. According to him, he was often joined by other residents on his walks. However, that day it was just the two of us. We circled on the pathway, walking and talking. When we became tired, he and I sat in the little alcove and continued to talk.

A little while later, the caregiver announced that the singing group Dad normally participated in was scheduled to meet in about 5 minutes. I said, "I'd like to sit in."

Dad was excited that I wanted to sing with him and his group.

Proudly, Dad walked with me to the place where we would be singing. He and I were the first ones to arrive. I noticed, the chairs were arranged in a circle and one of the leaders had placed song books on the seats of each chair. The song books were written in large print that appealed to the elderly residents.

As the other residents came into the room, a young lady, who was a little older than me wanted the chair I was sitting in. I was sitting next to Dad on his right side.

Evidently, she preferred that side of him as well. I suggested that she sit in the empty chair on Dad's left and she complied. I was still a little unnerved as I watched how she carefully interacted with Dad. I found out, that she and Dad enjoyed each other's company on more than one occasion. She flirted with him and kept him entertained, when I could not during the singing session. Obviously, he appreciated her comradery.

Dad's cataracts clouded his vision and he had glasses that hung around his neck so they could be easily placed over his eyes, but he rarely used them. He knew the words to most of the songs anyway and did not need the books. When he was asked to sing a song that he was not familiar to him, he simply hummed along with the music. When Dad sang it was in harmony. His tenor voice blended well with the other singers. I am not sure where he learned to sing perfect harmony or if he just faked it, but he always sang in key and I loved listening to him. I was not as talented as Dad and I simply sang the melody. Still, both of us sounded pretty good singing together and often we carried the tune for the rest of the group.

MEMORIES AND FORGETFULNESS

After the singing event, one of the caregivers came up to me afterward and acknowledged that Dad and this lady who was younger than him often talked together. She said, "I allow this to continue, but when your Mother comes, I remove the lady from your Dad's vicinity and your Mother is none the wiser." The care provider protected my mother from being jealous or humiliated.

***

In 2002, Marcella our middle daughter, left for Wisconsin to pursue a graduate degree. Before she left the west coast, she decided to visit grandparents in Seattle to say goodbye and enjoy their company. She relayed a conversation she had with my father who told her a war story. Dad explained that he would fly to various locations in France to deliver supplies to the troops who were near the front during World War II. Dad said, "We would often fly over the country trying to find a landing strip and then through the fog one would appear before we landed at the site." He hesitated for a long moment, looking like he contemplated saying something. Marcella said. "I didn't see signs of dementia. I was perplexed and continued listening for what came next." Then, Dad continued, "Somehow, we found those sites and landed safely every time."

Later, as Marcella retold the story, she wondered, "Maybe Grandpa hesitated because he thought about how his mind became foggy." Then rhetorically, she asked, "What gave him the ability to seek and to find the sites or for that matter deal with his dementia?" I did not have a good answer. Marcella asked and answered her own question, "I thought you may say—his faith in God."

In October of 2004, in Wisconsin, Marcella and her girlfriend came back to the west coast in order to hold a commitment ceremony in Medford, Oregon. We made elaborate arrangements to attend Marcella's function. Unlike our youngest daughter's wedding in Tacoma, nearly everyone needed to travel and stay overnight in Medford. I wanted my family in attendance, especially my father because now he stayed in a memory care facility. Carrie and I knew it would be difficult for Mother to care for Dad in a hotel. We confronted this dilemma by researching the owners of the memory care facility. They operated a similar unit in Medford. I inquired about an overnight stay for Dad at this facility and they were accommodating.

When we arrived at the Medford unit it was rather late. This was the night before the commitment ceremony. I made arrangements that included the time and day the staff could expect my father. Dad bounced up to the door like a kid going to a slumber party and he knocked. When the attendant opened the door, Dad walked through it and into the facility like he knew the place. I felt very comfortable leaving him there.

The next day, Mother and Dad arrived at the ceremony. Nervously, I watched Dad and tried to gauge his level of self-confidence. He seemed to respond okay, but I worried about his ability to follow directions. I assured myself that he would be in the proper place at the proper time. Brian and Jason, our sons-in-law, escorted the grandmothers to their seats. We expected Dad to follow Mother. Jason cradled Mothers arm and escorted her to her place. Like a trooper, Dad followed them at a respectful distance and did very well. All of the relatives were seated in the same area.

Dad made it through the event under Mother's

watchful eye. He held a song book steady for himself and her. Upon greeting Marcella after the ceremony Dad gave her a gentle kiss on the cheek and a larger than life smile as he congratulated his granddaughter on the accomplishment.

Mother and Dad left for Lake Forest Park after the ceremony and did not stay for the reception or a second night. Still, I was happy that my parents attended the ceremony and it turned out well.

***

One weekend after Marcella's event in Medford, I came up to Seattle to visit Dad. My brother Steve and I went without Mother to the Lake Forest Park memory care facility. We walked into the unit as normal, but Dad was not in his room. I went to the activity room and asked the caregiver, "Where is my Dad?" He did not know but said he would look for him. I did not see the caregiver again. About 10 to 15 minutes later I saw Dad. He walked toward Steve and me, down the opposite wing of the facility to the activity room where we waited. He was dressed in other people's garments that overlaid his clothes. His hair looked like it had not been combed for a while and the disheveled look helped explain his puzzled nature as he walked up to us. His eyes were downcast. Obviously, he had been caught by surprise.

I do not think Steve dared say anything provocative. He was extraordinarily quiet and followed my lead.

I am not sure Dad recognized Steve or me or possibly he wanted to avoid us altogether. It was a disconcerting moment for me and likely Steve too. I tried to accept the situation. I greeted Dad with a happy, "Hi Dad," and we began our afternoon visit together. Steve helped me escort Dad back to his room. We talked on the way but I could tell he was not interested in having a long conversation.

I suggested that we go to the park and he reluctantly agreed. I helped him change into appropriate clean clothes. We found his comb and he ran it through his hair.

As we were getting ready to leave, he moved from one foot to another like a little kid who had to go to the bathroom. So, I suggested we go to the men's room. Dad and I walked into his restroom across from his bedroom. I went to a stall and he to the urinal. I do not know what happened, but he walked out. I wondered if Dad had really felt an urge to use the toilet.

I learned from caregivers that Dad suffered from incontinence. They told me that he had relieved himself elsewhere in the facility. He could no longer manage himself and needed extra care.

As I tried to find Dad in the hallway outside the bathroom, I discovered a chair with a wet cushion and a puddle on the floor underneath the chair. I did not know the cause of the accident, but I offered to clean it up. A caregiver insisted he would take care of the situation. I thanked him and went to Dad's room where I found Steve and him waiting for me. Quietly, we left and went out for our daily adventure.

A couple of weeks later on another visit, Dad and I planned to go to a different park. On the way, I needed some personal items like deodorant, and I thought Dad might enjoy going to the store with me. The store was on the way. As we entered the store we walked down the aisle, he lagged behind. He would stop and look at an item on the shelf and thoroughly examine the article. I feared he may not replace the item where he had found it or alternatively place the piece in his pocket. I tried the best I could to encourage him to keep up with me but still he lagged behind. Although, I just wanted to obtain my merchandise, pay for it and leave, Dad continued to stop and look at things along the way. I stayed with him looking at the items too, not making much progress toward the deodorant.

Then, something unconventional even for Dad happened. He spit saliva into a corner under the endcap of one of the aisles. Initially, I thought I would ignore it but then decided to say something.

I looked at him and said, "Dad, please don't do that." Without a beat, he said, "Its okay. Nobody cares."

Dad's response was totally out of character. I did not explain that this was inappropriate behavior because I did not think he would learn from the situation.

Instead, I abandoned my search for deodorant and

simply said, "Let's go to the park."

If Dad could have witnessed this incident now from the vantage point of ten years earlier, he would have been horrified at what he did and said. I realized how much *the dementia* was stealing him from me.

Slowly, I grasped conceptually, that he had taken another step down in his mental capacities. At first, I realized that he had a hard time figuring out locations and how to get from one place to another. Also, I noticed he had a hard time solving problems. He hesitated more and he seemed confused on how to do simple tasks.

As an example, one day he could not nest grocery carts in a store. He made several attempts before my daughter, Hettie, said, "That's okay Grandpa, sometimes I have difficulty with that too," and she helped him nest the cart.

Additionally, when surroundings changed, he found it difficult to keep his moral compass. His doctor told us he suspected a TIA (Transient Ischemic Attack) or a minor stroke had occurred and each event made a significant change in his life. These steps down in his abilities could be either subtle or more pronounced.

Some days, Dad seemed to adjust just fine to his surroundings. However, on other days, he definitely was lost and not alert to his setting and the people in his life. It appeared to me that he became more self-absorbed and less concerned about others needs or their welfare.

Before, he would have displayed a feeling of guilt or his sense of duty would challenge any impropriety. Now, Dad was not aware he was creating additional work for others or behaving in a manner that did not conform to normal standards. Previously, my father maintained a strong sense of awareness about people and his impact on others. That side of him had faded and at certain times had vanished entirely. It seemed to me his condition was getting worse.

In addition, to the incontinence and disruptive behavior, the management at the memory care facility suggested to Mother that she find another place for Dad. Mother was thoughtful about the move. One day, she announced that she had found another facility that was close to her house.

FAILING MEMORY

She moved Dad to a senior living center that also had an Alzheimer's and memory care wing. I was impressed by the facility. That unit of the center was located on the first floor behind locked doors which had been updated with modern fixtures and lighting. Each individual's room was larger than the previous one, but it housed fewer residents than the other memory care facility. The large dining area included a large glass windows that looked out on a nice patio area with a garden. Dad's room had a brightly lit bathroom that was attached.

Mom suspected that Dad did not like using the bathroom at the former memory care facility due to the "closed-in" feeling he had and the poor lighting. Mom lived and shopped in the neighborhood and she could visit him frequently.

After about a month, I visited Dad a second time with Mother. The manager of the unit requested to see Mother. She and I walked into the manager's office. He sat down and explained Dad's progress. It stunned me, when he suggested that we must find another place for Dad. The manager explained that this facility was not a good fit for him. He would not put Dad out on the street. However, he needed more care than this facility could provide and suggested that we contact a nursing home or an adult family home living facility. I was distraught. Our hope that this place would have been the right one for Dad evaporated.

I walked into see Dad, who had a welcoming air about him. Mother took him down to the dining area to talk. I told mother I would get a sweater for Dad, because sometimes he became cold when he was in the dining area.

In the dining area, I found Dad and Mother. I gave Dad the comb and kept the sweater close by incase he complained or simply wanted to wear it. While Dad combed his hair, Mother said she wanted to go back and talk to the manager. I stayed with Dad and we generated a pleasant conversation about his new home, what I accomplished at work, how my siblings were doing and other topics of interest. Dad appeared to be restless and not interested in our conversation. After a short while, he did not want to engage at all. I suspected Dad had lost interest in most things and that included being with family. Although, he seemed to understand our conversation, I developed a sense that I needed to keep him entertained and sadly realized that he had taken another step down in mental awareness.

On the way out of the senior living home, I articulated my observation about Dad's downward steps and expressed my concern to Mother about him taking another step in the wrong direction if we found a third facility. Others told me, research shows changing facilities can have a dramatic effect on patients with dementia. Mother acknowledged my concern and said, "We have no choice." The health provider gave Mother a list of adult care homes and nursing facilities to review.

Mother and I took the next day and visited a number of homes trying to find a good match for Dad. It was a frustrating and troubling experience. We made the best of our time, hoping for better results. So, I came up to visit Mother the following weekend and we looked at additional homes. My mother relied on my help and as difficult as it was for me, I was happy to aid her. It was hard trying to find the best fit for Dad and helping Mother make the decision where she was going to house my father.

CHAPTER 18 – ADULT CARE HOME

My father and mother enrolled in a special medical insurance patient care program when they first moved to the Seattle Area. I was a toddler at that time. It was modeled after the European healthcare systems. The company offered an insurance plan that included its own medical providers, hospitals and pharmacies. The insurance coverage provided doctors, nurses and personnel to assist with medical concerns to keep healthcare costs low. They accepted patients through their own Medicare Advantage Program where payments were made to the parent company. This form of insurance proved to be effective and much cheaper than the traditional Medicare and supplemental programs.

As far as I know, the health care program originated in the Seattle area and merged with another organization from California several years ago. The doctors who choose work in this program or the confines of the organization made referrals to other doctors within their network. There were exceptions that occurred, but generally speaking those who used this plan accepted the diagnosis, outcomes and results. The doctors all seemed to be passionate about the ideas of providing quality care for their patients.

After conducting our exhaustive search, one weekend, Mother and I settled on an adult care home in Lake Forest Park for Dad. It was on the list of facilities that the insurance company recommended. The owner operated two houses about ½ mile up the road from where Mother lived. You could walk up the hill and knock on the door, although normally we drove the short distance. One of the homes was large and presumably housed her family and had several lady boarders who needed care around the clock. The house overlooked Lake Washington with a gorgeous view of the water and an opportunity to see sea planes land at the local air harbor. This was similar to the view from Mother's house. Another smaller home that was located on the same property, was where the owner's parents lived; a mother-in-law's house per se. Another dwelling was just up the hill and next-door. This was another adult memory care home and had a large semi-circular driveway leading to the house, with a huge fir tree between the drive and the roadway. The owner offered a room in this house to Dad, which also was a residence for a lady who had her own bedroom.

The owner, who was a nurse, worked for the company that offered the medical insurance plan and was studying to become a nurse practitioner. She hired a second nurse who also stayed in the house where Dad lived. The owner's father, a retired doctor, enjoyed a quiet life and helped his daughter when it was necessary.

Mother chose this adult care home because it offered full time nursing services. The proximity of the owner's house to the homes on the property meant she would keep close watch on my father and each resident's needs in a timely fashion. In addition, the owner hired other caregivers during the day to come in and get residents up and dressed in the morning, cook their meals, clean the house and entertain them. Since Mother's house was close to the place that was caring for Dad, she attempted a trip to see him at least once a day. They would talk and take short walks around the neighborhood. Mother could not walk far herself, so short walks were as much as she could manage. Also, she feared that he may fall and this prevented her from taking him out of the immediate surroundings. Most importantly, if something happened to Dad she would need help that the caregivers could provide.

When I came to Lake Forest Park, I made a point to spend as much time as I could with my father. Often, Carrie dropped me off and then she would travel south to see her father and siblings. Alva, my sister, and her husband, Ted, were now living in California. My brother, Steve, owned a condominium but stayed with Mother at the old homestead for much of the time. Mother appreciated the company. Steve often accompanied Mother to see Dad. She would read to him, play the organ or sing songs for entertainment. When Steve came to visit, he read to him from the Bible or wheeled him outside to walk around the neighborhood. Mike, my second brother, would visit Dad on the weekends or whenever he could find the time. Mike worked long hours on his job. When he had some free time he spent it raising his family of five children. Although, he remained busy, he always found time to visit and sing or read to

FAILING MEMORY

Dad.

Once again, Dad's mental capacities stepped down. During the day, caregivers would place Dad in front of a huge TV screen which he watched in the common area. If they turned on the soap operas and allowed him to watch the shows while they fixed meals or cleaned the house, Dad would become completely engrossed in the programs, take on the personality of one of the characters and start yelling at the TV. It seemed as if he embodied the personalities of the characters of the programs he watched. Evidently, the dementia allowed him to no longer feel inhibited. Mother recognized this issue and suggested that the caregivers keep Dad in his bedroom. They allowed him to watch shows on a small 13 inch TV. He could easily relate to his surroundings and realize the entertainment value of the programs without always thrusting himself into the characters.

I visited Dad once or twice a month in order to spend weekends with him. If Mother needed something I would travel to the Seattle Area and spend any necessary time with her. Since, I moved to The Dalles and later to Umatilla, driving to Lake Forest Park became a matter of a 3-4 hour road trip. I drove all over Oregon for my job; therefore this seemed like a snap and I rarely hesitated to make the trip.

I brought my guitar so that we could sing songs, work on puzzles, look at photos, read books, and anything else I could think of to entertain Dad. Also, we took walks. Dad's world had turned quite small. He had a series of medical issues that required the caregivers to monitor him on a regular basis.

Dad talked less. He could not form words and it became difficult to carry on a two way conversation with him. I assumed he comprehended what I said, but it became increasingly clear that his memory and mental abilities had faded. It became harder to spend more than a couple of hours with him. On days when it was not raining, Dad and I would walk around the block. It extended about a quarter mile to the north, then a short distance to the next road over, a quarter mile down that street to the south and then the short block back to the beginning and entrance to his adult care home. We walked slowly, observing whatever flowers we saw along the way, spotted birds in the trees, commented on the neighbor's new construction projects or obvious idiosyncrasies of each home along the way. When we arrived at a break in the trees where we could see Lake Washington, we stopped and both of us observed the boats on the water or the sea planes landing on the water and commented on their appearance.

The thing I enjoyed most about my visits with Dad, was the time we would sing songs together. Although, he did not talk much now, he would sing or hum along with me as I played the guitar. I enjoyed my one person audience because he always seemed interested and participated in the songs. When he sang, it was still in harmony as I carried the melody. He belted out the old church songs as he did when I was a kid. At first he knew many of the words, but as time went on he would just hum the harmony.

On Saturday, I would spend most of my day with him and on Sunday I would stop by in the morning for a half hour or hour to sing. Depending on how I felt, we would sing older folk songs.

When I was a child, about 1959, Dad preformed in

a community play where he was the lead character. In the play his character wanted to propose to his girlfriend whose name was Daisy. Then, he kissed her on stage, asked her to marry him and sang a song.

I sung one of his favorite songs from the play with him all these years later. We laughed when we finished singing. I do not know if he remembered the play or not, but I did and that was all that mattered to me.

As the months went by, Dad's mental aptitude took more steps downward. In 2006, Mother, Steve and I took Dad to see his doctor who specialized in geriatric care. He had seen Dad since about 1997 when he first was diagnosed with vascular dementia. Dad declined to the point where he did not talk and we knew he needed additional help. Also, he stopped singing, but still hummed. Mom called him the "big hummer." Dad had been taking medicine for memory maintenance, but his outbursts at the TV and his demonstration of other signs of agitation seemed to be cause for concern and let us know the medicine might not be working. The doctor told Mother and me that we just needed to look at my father and determine the best course of action for him, because he could not tell us. The doctor prescribed medicine that was supposed to stabilize the changes in Dad's moody behavior and limit any outbursts. That did not work well because he became clumsy and could not walk. Then, the doctor prescribed medicine that was designed to calm Dad's nerves and another to help with potential depression. Finally, through the use of different medicines, as well as trial and error, Dad's irrational behavior along with his outbursts subsided.

Since, the medications helped to stabilize Dad's behavior, his reactions and interactions with family and medical staff seemed better.

In the interim, as the doctor adjusted Dad's medications, the nursing staff at the owner's adult care home gave him a wheelchair and we purchased a lift. This device helped to get Dad in and out of bed, as well as his wheelchair with ease. The owner, who by now received her nurse practitioner license, talked to us about having Dad walk again. She knew that if he stayed in the wheelchair too long, he would never walk because frankly speaking, he would forget how to walk.

MEMORIES AND FORGETFULNESS

So, Mom, Steve and I and many times Mike, would follow the physical therapist's recommendations, by having Dad practice walking again. Dad walked up and down the hallway at the care home when two people helped him. One of us would encourage Dad to stand and walk along beside him. It was necessary to hold on to Dad by the belt that was around his waist. The other person followed behind with the wheelchair so that if he got tired he could sit down immediately. I helped every time I came to visit, but on most occasions Steve and Mom or Steve and the caregiver, or the caregiver and Mom would help Dad walk. We tried for several months, but eventually it became onerous for anyone of us to help Dad walk. Eventually, he did not want to try, and we gave up. Dad never walked again.

The medications that finally stabilized Dad's moods and gave him the ability to function, were mixed by the staff in some pudding and placed on a spoon. Dad would take the spoon, carefully turn it around, look at it, then turn it upside down, right-side up and eventually put it in his mouth to sample the medicine infused pudding. I was amazed to see the pudding stay on the spoon as he twirled it slowly, like it was a lollipop. He wanted to see all sides before placing it in his mouth.

For the most part, the caregivers fed Dad Asian dishes. The majority of the staff were from the Philippines. That was the owner's family's origin. Dad liked different foods and never complained. Graciously, he accepted the meals and ate whatever the caregivers placed in front of him. However, he ate less now, and it was unclear to me whether he was tired of the food or simply was not hungry. Slowly, his weight decreased.

One day, Mother told me, "I know he is declining and I see his deterioration daily. I have conversations with God about what to do. I don't like to see him suffer like this." In her own way, she told me she had been thinking about Dad and wondering when...

In 2008, Dad stopped humming altogether. He barely made a sound and became less and less aware of his surroundings. When I visited, I still took him for walks, but during these times I walked by pushing him around the block in his wheelchair. We talked about the same things, but I did all the talking. He was silent, but in his silence he still had his moments of awareness. The owner had an organ in the house and Mother sat at the organ and played songs; mainly hymns, while Dad simply listen. Mom played for hours and in her quiet way communed with my father.

When I discussed my father's situation with friends or relatives, they questioned me and asked, "Does your father know who you are?" The question surprised me, and my response came naturally, "It doesn't matter to me. What I am sure of, is that my father knows I am there and that I love him. That is all that matters."

Especially, later on, I realized I needed to be with Dad whenever I could. I felt determined to be in his presence, even if just for a short visit. Every once in a while, I would see a glimmer of hope in Dad's eyes or a small improvement in his abilities. It was never anything very great, but it gave me hope. I saw God at work giving him small blessings, given his current state. While Dad suffered with dementia, facing darkness and day to day dreariness, sometimes he would make a profound statement with his actions, or acknowledge the people in the room with such openness or happiness, that at times I felt he truly loved in a childlike way. Sometimes, a simple calmness came over my father, like an acceptance of his situation, like an acceptance of God and his current life. I felt like God bestowed mercy on him. Maybe it was the medication, maybe it was acceptance, but the agitation he had earlier in his dementia seemed to be gone. He seemed content.

I would tear up as I would sing hymns to him.

One day my mother told Marcella, my daughter, "Grandpa is now on earth to love and be loved." Indeed it seemed to be true.

***

Emma, my youngest daughter, came from Arizona to visit Dad one day in the spring of 2008. She brought her son Bernie with her. He was not even a year old. I took him with me to the back porch of the home where Dad, Bernie and I sat in the shade, looking out on the sun-filled backyard. The caregiver placed a blanket over Dad to keep him warm and shelter him from the light breeze that blew that day. I handed baby Bernie to Dad and placed him in his lap so he could hold his great grandson. As Dad held him he felt the significance of the event, because he tried to smile. Dad did not smile much anymore and the muscles in his face did not work like they did at one time. It was hard to tell if the facial expression was a grimace or a smile, but based on his demeanor and based on what I knew about my father, it had to be a smile. He felt satisfied and happy.

When Emma talked to Dad, I told her to tell my father what she did for a living. She had graduated in 2006 with her teacher's certificate and Master's Degree in Education. She told him she taught physics at an Arizona High School. When I said, "You inspired her, Dad, with your teaching career." He teared up with happiness and satisfaction, but did not say a word.

Just before Christmas in November 2008, Mike and I went to visit Dad. When he stopped humming along with the songs, I knew he was not enjoying life as much. The caregivers had gotten him out of bed, placed him in his wheelchair and moved him to the living room. When we arrived "that" morning, I pulled out my guitar. We sang a few Christmas songs, and then Mike said he wanted to sing a special song for Dad. I put down my guitar and let Mike sing it a cappella. He began, like an opera singer, with his deep round throated voice.

Dad watched and listened intently.

Toward the last part of the Christmas song, Mike's voice built itself into a crescendo and he struck a high note that rattled the curtains and the paintings on the wall. Dad let out a loud joyful cry! It sounded like Dad was in pain but he was not suffering. He was enjoying the performance. It was at that moment, Mike stopped singing because he was thinking something was seriously wrong. I motioned for him to continue. Dad emotions were caught up in the sound of Mike's voice and the song he was singing. Dad must have thought about the angels, the beauty of the song he heard, the sinking to his knees and that night knowing Christ was about to be born.

As Mike finished the song, his voice trailed off and Dad sat still with tears streaming down both cheeks. Mike had sang a glorious rendition of the carol and he nailed the song; perfectly.

We both came to Dad and put our arms around

him, hugged him tightly and wept too.

FAILING MEMORY

CHAPTER 19 -- 2009

It was Tuesday, February 3, 2009. Carrie and I flew into Seattle. We were returning from a delightful mini-vacation; an extended weekend of sorts in Arizona. A couple of years prior to this date, we purchased a house with Carrie's father near Emma in Mesa, Arizona and tried to use Arizona as our vacation location as time allowed. This was especially true in the winter. At this time, I worked in Hermiston, Oregon and Seattle was a 4 hour ride from our home. It was easy to fly from Phoenix to Seattle and visit family that lived in both locations.

When I got the call from Alva, my sister, we had just arrived back in Seattle from Phoenix and had finished a visit with Carrie's family. We were leaving for Hermiston, when the phone rang. Also, at that time, Alva was visiting Mother and Dad from Riverside, California where she lived.

It was shocking news, but not unexpected, when my sister told me Dad was in the hospital with pneumonia. I told Carrie about the call and let her know that I wanted to stay near Dad. She agreed wholeheartedly. We both made arrangements with our respective employers and dashed out of the West Seattle condominium of my father-in-law's to head to Bellevue.

At some point, I anticipated receiving a call that would let me know something was seriously wrong with Dad, but I had put those thoughts out of my mind. His struggle with dementia worsened and we knew the disease itself would not cause his death, necessarily, but there may be other complications. We just did not know the form. I remained hopeful despite the fact Dad was not talking or walking, or eating and now he had pneumonia.

During that overcast day, which is typical for Seattle, I did not need to say much to Carrie. Mostly, we drove in silence to Bellevue. We traveled on I-90 over the old floating bridge south of Bellevue. Everything seemed to be a blur to me. However, I oriented myself to my surroundings. My focus was like that of a laser as I went about the task of finding the medical center.

The hospital was located right off Interstate 405, on the right hand side of the freeway; like I remembered.

FAILING MEMORY

I figured out how to exit the freeway and work my way to the hospital. We wandered around the streets trying to find the best place to park. I was rattled, when I stopped the car at a convenience store and asked a clerk for directions to the hospital entrance. The clerk told me, but I promptly forgot, except for the vague notion of "over there;" remembering she pointed her finger. Carrie and I walked briskly toward the hospital to what I thought was the entrance. We wandered, somewhat aimlessly, through the hallways until I found the guest service desk. They explained where to find the elevator.

We took the south tower elevator up to the fourth floor and asked for Dad's room number at the nurse's station. I met my siblings and Mother just outside Dad's room. My family updated me on Dad's condition and confirmed that he had pneumonia. He was lying quietly in his bed, connected to an IV and receiving a saline solution. The nurse explained to us that they had intended to stabilize Dad until he could be seen by his doctor.

Further, Alva told us, "Dad had not eaten a full meal for several days and a staff member at the adult care home called 911 to take him to the hospital." She went on, "I walked in, sat down beside his bed, and told Dad we arrived, and that we all loved him very much and wanted him to get better. I told him he was in the hospital and in a good place and will be well taken care of. I said, Larry will be here shortly."

Carrie had work in the morning and needed to head back home. Alva agreed to chauffer me around the Seattle area.

Mom said, "Your Dad is resting comfortably and is out of danger." As we waited for the doctor to arrive to provide us with her assessment, my siblings made observations about Dad that focused on how he looked, what happened upon his arrival and stated Dad was resting peacefully in the room nearby.

Then, Mom said, "Larry you should go in and see him."

I walked into the hospital room with an urgency in my step. There was the clean smell of disinfectant in contrasted to the stark and plain surroundings. I walked up to his bed and said, "Dad, I'm here. I love you and I am staying over another night." I explained that I had just returned from a trip to Arizona.

"I couldn't wait to come to the hospital just to see you."

He woke for a moment and acknowledged my presence with his eyes and made an attempt to smile. I could tell, he still felt lousy and could not or would not express it one way or another. He just laid there, mostly motionless and speechless. I grabbed his hand and sat there in silence with him for a while.

The hospital had assigned Dad a room that was located on the west side. It was a spacious unadorned room with a stiff sitting couch for guests. The couch was near to a large window, from which you could see the freeway. The beige wallpaper seemed to help create a peaceful place when you compared Dad's room to the hustle and bustle of nurses and doctors walking up and down the hallway. I saw a busy world outside Dad's hospital room.

I was struck by the stark contrast that existed in Dad's world of relative quietness and serenity and the one that functioned on the other side of his bedroom door. This included the cars on the freeway I viewed from his window.

When the geriatric doctor arrived, I excused myself saying, "Dad, I want to talk to the doctor."

My siblings, Mother and I gathered around the doctor. I asked her, "What treatment plan do you have for Dad?" We all expected him to easily kick the pneumonia and get back to living at the adult care home. We knew doctors regularly prescribed medicine that cured pneumonia and it seemed to us that Dad could simply take an antibiotic or some such pill and get better.

The doctor, somewhat defensively, explained Dad's desire was that no heroic measures be taken to save his life. At this stage of his medical condition, Dad wanted his body to travel a "natural course." The hospital had a "no added measures document" on file that Dad had signed. He did not want to be on life support of any type. Further, she explained what we already knew. Dad would probably remain immobile and continue to depend on caregivers at this aspect of his life. The documents clearly reflected what we knew, but in the moment forgot.

Many years before Dad had dementia, he made it clear to Mother that he did not want tubes stuck in him to help him cling to life without hope of ultimate recovery. At this point, Mom recalled a vivid memory of the time when she and Dad were at her cousin's, Fred's, bedside in the hospital. He had a breathing apparatus, an IV, a catheter and a feeding tube in him as he lay immobilized and restrained during his end of life illness. Dad unambiguously commented to Mother, "I DO NOT want that stuff hanging off of me when I get to that point." Dad's disgust and repulsion during that event returned to Mother. Her voice was intense when she spoke because the realization of being confronted with Dad's end of life care was daunting. Mother knew the answer. The health care instructions clearly stated Dad's expectations.

After sharing Dad's file with us, the doctor suggested hospice. She explained how hospice worked, why it was appropriate and how hospice aligned with his wishes.

I only remember the jolt that I felt and it took

several minutes for me to process the fact that my father's journey had come to an end. I was frustrated, as I thought about my father, who could receive simple care and did not have to die.

At the time, I knew my father's strong beliefs must prevail. I could hear him ask, "What kind of life would I have anyway?" My responsibility to him changed direction instantaneously and drastically. The hospital was no longer the place for him.

Immediately, the doctor recognized how devastated I was after hearing her words about Dad's condition and she empathized with me. It was not her place to offer the last word. So, she explained that we could place Dad at a convalescence center that was just down the road. They would encourage Dad to eat and give him every chance to continue his life.

The doctor observed our comportment and it sent a signal to her that we still needed a little more convincing. She started to give us more options by saying, "He looks like he is resting peacefully now and the IV is doing its job." She continued, "You could leave him here in the hospital, let him regain his strength and offer him antibiotics." That snapped me back into reality. I uttered, "No," somewhat under my breath when the doctor suggested antibiotics. It pained me to think of him continuing to live without speaking or walking as much as it pained me to put him in hospice. My siblings and Mother also had a similar reaction to mine but did not verbalize what they were thinking.

I said, "I'm convinced Dad did not want to continue to live like this." He was certainly tired of his life the way it was now and he was not going to get better. A productive life entailed communicating and being a mobile person. He did not communicate and relied on a wheelchair for mobility. We knew Dad's answer. His answer became the kindest and most generous decision that we could select.

We needed to make a final unbearable resolution; one we could not go back and change. It became a decision for him and not with him. He could not communicate with us. He did not have the problem solving abilities anymore. He took life minute by minute accepting whatever came his way.

MEMORIES AND FORGETFULNESS

When I composed myself, I said, "So, I guess this is it then." Alva and Mike both said, "Yes, I guess it is." Mom in her own way agreed reiterating, "I guess we have our answer." Steve was not convinced and it still bothered him that we contemplated hospice. With the exception of Steve's reluctance, I think we all felt backed into a corner and needed to honor Dad's wishes. Even Steve finally agreed.

We continued to discuss the upcoming circumstances. Should we take the doctor's recommendation of a new convalescence center or should we stick with the current adult care home? In the end, with input from the owner, we decided to return Dad to his present situation under hospice.

The owner, who was a nurse practitioner, explained to us, "We do hospice here and your father is familiar with our home and how we do things. I don't think it is a good idea for you to move him to another facility. If you're going to put him in hospice and have him live out his days in a familiar environment, keep him here." That became our final decision.

FAILING MEMORY

We planned to talk more in the morning, as we were all exhausted. For now, Dad would stay in the hospital tonight. I was not about to let Dad spend a night in an unfamiliar hospital room alone, so I decided to stay with him. When I told my family I planned to spend the night with Dad, they agreed with me and headed to their respective homes. Alva said, "I'll be back tomorrow to pick you up." I was relieved because most major decisions had been made. The hospital arranged for an ambulance to take Dad back to the adult care home the next day.

I settled in the best I could, on the hard couch, next to the window in his room with Dad in the hospital bed near me. I did not sleep much that night but gladly I spent the time listening to him breathe. The sound of his systematic but raking breath in the bed on the other side of the room was a comfort to me as I closed my eyes and tried to fall asleep. Continuously, I woke up throughout the night, stared at the moon and stars out the big hospital window or watched the big rig trucks go up and down the freeway. I listened to the roar of their engines.

Periodically, a nurse would come into the room to

check on Dad. About 10 p.m. there was a shift change. A nurse came into the room and said in a loud voice, "Heeay!" Obviously, she was good natured and this engendered a lovely way about her. Dad responded and smiled like he had always done in the past. In a cheery and as natural as could be voice he returned the greeting with, "Heeay!" Gladly, I witnessed this joyful noise that came from my father as I watched him return the greeting. It seemed he actually did feel a little better, if only for a moment. This pleased me, because the nurse had treated Dad like he was a valuable patient in the hospital. Her simple act made my father's day, because it had been the only word I had heard him utter for a complete year.

However, the joy I felt was short lived and ceased as the nurse began to work. She changed Dad, his sheets and checked his vital signs. The IV in Dad's arm twisted and turned and he winced because it must have hurt. He did not cry out in pain, but just a grimace on his face told me that he had held back a painful response. As the nurse continued to work in an efficient manner, it became obvious to me that my father viewed what she was doing as a nuisance. When she left, he lay there in silence relieved, but still groping with the aftermath of what had occurred.

The following morning, after a change in shifts, another nurse came into the room. The nurse was either told or had convinced herself that my father needed a catheter. I do not know why, but for whatever reason, she came in and said, "I am here to put a catheter in your father." I stated, "I don't think he wants one. You can try but he's not going to like it." I wish I had been more forthright and forceful because my response did not even satisfy me.

She ignored me and started preparations to put the catheter in him. I left the room. When I came back in after a few moments, she smiled and said, "He's strong. I wasn't able to put the catheter in him. He fought me all the way." As I expected.

Thinking back, I kicked myself for not being a better advocate for him by being more direct and saying, "Don't put that thing in him. He doesn't want it." It would have spared him the anguish of fighting her off.

MEMORIES AND FORGETFULNESS

That morning, I spent a great deal of time talking to Dad. I was trying to reassure him by talking about the plans that we had made. He was scheduled to leave the hospital today and return to his adult care home. It was the place where he had spent the last 3-4 years of his life.

I wanted to state to him that I would take him home to the bed he had spent much of his life in; at his homestead. But, I could not say that to him. There would not have been the needed, familiar caregivers and the bed that he had become accustomed to at this time. I just hoped he would understand. Yet, to this day I still keep the guilt about the end of my father's life in my mind. As Carrie often says, "You did the best for your father with the information that you had at the time and there is nothing to feel guilty about." Still, the guilty feeling persists.

Later in the morning, Alva and Mom returned to the hospital. After my call to Carrie, she also returned to Lake Forest Park. Steve and Mike said they intended to meet us at the adult care home when Dad arrived. It took forever for Dad to be discharged. He rested peacefully on his back. This was a saving grace. His hoarse breathing continued; in then out, as he scavenged for enough air. He kept his mouth open and took in all the air he could with each breath. Sometimes, he stopped breathing and my attention went straight to him, wondering if it would be his last. But, invariably, a big intake of air would occur and he would breathe out a deep breath and his raspy breathing would continue through his mouth.

The doctor arrived in the late morning and finalized Dad's discharge from the hospital. The ambulance company was notified that Dad was leaving and it took several hours before it arrived. Dad continued to rest. The nurse came in to his room and removed the IV from his arm. The paramedics arrived to transport Dad to his adult care home.

The paramedics placed Dad onto a gurney, wheeled him into the elevator and to the ambulance that was awaiting. I saw one of the paramedics aim a light down Dad's throat to assure that his breathing pathways stayed open. I was told, Dad slept through much of the transport. They planned for the worst but I was also impressed that they took great care with my father. I appreciated that level of medical care. Although, it seemed ironic in a way that they took so much care with him when we expected Dad to die naturally.

The ambulance had room for the driver and only one paramedic in the vehicle with my father. The driver and her partner readied themselves to leave for the address they were given. Alva and I prepared to leave as well. I yearned to get back to more familiar surroundings.

The winter day darkness hit me as I walked outside. Finally, Alva and I arrived at the car. We drove north toward the adult care home. We began driving by following behind the ambulance. But then, the ambulance driver took a different turn than I expected. She decided to cross the Evergreen Floating Bridge across Lake Washington into Seattle proper. You can get to Lake Forest Park going through Seattle, but it seemed like a long meandering route instead of a straightforward one. I figured they knew what they were doing or if they did not Dad would get a nice comfortable ride someplace and eventually the paramedics would find their way to his care home. Instead of continuing to drive behind the paramedics, we drove up Interstate 405 on the east side of the lake to Bothell then west to Lake Forest Park like we had done many times in the past. I knew we would beat the ambulance to the Lake Forest Park home and we did.

Once I arrived, I went inside to talk to the caregiver and let her know Dad would arrive soon. I waited for him and the ambulance for what seemed like hours, but it was just about a half hour later when the ambulance pulled up to the driveway and the paramedics wheeled him into the home. He was resting comfortably but still had the coarse rasping sound of his breathing seeking air. The caregiver lifted Dad into his bed and tucked him in for the evening. Easily, he fell back to sleep and continued his melodic breathing.

The insurance coverage included the services of a hospice social worker and nurse. They were scheduled to stop by Dad's home around 7 p.m. and talk to the family. Carrie and Mom arrived at the care home at about the same time, then later Steve, Mike and Alva joined us. We all arrived about 6:30 p.m. in preparation to meet with the hospice workers. We talked about our expectations and Carrie explained how hospice meetings normally evolve. She worked for hospice in Oregon for several years.

While we waited for the hospice workers to appear, I suggested that my siblings and I take shifts at Dad's bedside for the nighttime. I wanted a comforting face near Dad should he wake or pass during the night. We agreed that Steve would take the first shift from 9-12 a.m. since Steve normally stayed up that late anyway, Mike would watch Dad between 12-6 a.m. because he knew it would be one of the toughest shifts and I would relieve him at 6. I did not know how long we would need to continue this vigil, so I prepared myself to do my part no matter what happened.

Carrie and I had a similar experience with her mother. In 2005, Carrie's mom was in the hospital dying from cancer and her family members took turns staying in the room with her. For several days and nights Carrie's mother was not alone. I admired Carrie and her family's tenacity during that time. I wanted the same thing for my Dad. He would not be alone either.

I am very glad that my mother and siblings wholeheartedly agreed with the concept of a vigil to be with my father.

The hospice workers came at 7 p.m. and explained the process to us. They discussed the role that the family plays in making a loved one comfortable as nature takes its course. Should something happen, hospice must to be called first; not 911. Hospice is used for the person who is only expected to live 6 months or less. There are exceptions. Sometimes people rally and beat the 6 months prediction. Anything could become possible and we held onto our hopes.

Dad changed his shallow raking breathing ever so slightly and I asked his nurse what it meant. She got up, went to the bed to watch Dad for a moment and then came back to us. She said, "It sounds like the last vestiges of life. This is called chain-stoking which is a normal part of the dying process." My heart fell when I heard her words, although I expected this to occur.

The gravity of the nurse's statement hit me hard. I recall the interminable moment of silence that fell on the initial meeting the family had with hospice officials when we discussed Dad's situation.

MEMORIES AND FORGETFULNESS

I guess this is what they meant by *hospice*. It became real. When the meeting concluded, the nurse provided us with clear instructions for Dad's care and how we should handle everything from day to day or if necessary for months. At this point, no one expected Dad to be with us for more than a number of days. We shared contact information, gave each other hugs and said our goodbyes. The hospice workers left us with our thoughts and plans.

Alva, Mike, Carrie and Mom departed. Steve and I stayed. I wanted to give Steve some moral support for his upcoming shift. I told him I would leave around 10 p.m. I planned to walk to Mom's house and see everyone in the morning. Steve and I sat in Dad's room, quietly talking as he slept. It was important for us to stay with Dad. Gently, I held his hand and watched his breathing with my brother.

At 11:30 p.m. my younger brother Mike, returned to the adult care home. I was pleasantly surprised to see him so early. I updated Mike on Dad's condition and told him how grateful I was for his presence. I checked in with Mike to determine if he still wanted to complete his shift tonight and he assured me, "I will call you if there is any significant change in Dad's condition." He said, "Go get some rest Larry." With a grateful look in my eyes, I said "Thank you."

I said, "Let's go Steve, you can drive me to Mom's." Steve responded with his cheery, "Okay," and we left. We got back to the homestead and Steve went to his bedroom. I went to bed and tried to fall asleep with my phone nearby. I did not want to wake Mother who was in the next room slumbering away. I was keyed up and tossed and turned for a while, but then dozed off.

At 2:15 a.m., the phone rang. It was Mike. I thanked him for calling. He said Dad passed. It was February 5, 2009 at roughly 2:00 a.m. when Dad took his last breath. Mike called hospice as he had been instructed. The caregiver on staff at the adult care home called the owner. I woke Mom and Steve. I called Alva, then drove to the adult care home. We were all blurry eyed and tried to think of the instructions we had been given by the hospice workers. Slowly, we began to make arrangements through the funeral home and other contacts that were required.

MEMORIES AND FORGETFULNESS

I thanked Mike for being there with Dad and said, "Mike I can't tell you how much I appreciate you and I am very grateful for what you have done." I continued, "I couldn't have hoped for a better person to be with Dad at his last breath." Mike teared up and said "Dad was my hero." I said, "He was a hero to us all." Mike replied, "When Dad passed, I gave a little prayer to urge him on his way."

Dad was out of pain and no longer needed to fight his dementia. Dad, always the hero to our family did not have to suffer any longer. We believed he could fly now with the angels and he entered a much better place. Also, silently and briefly I said a prayer to the God I believed in. I asked,

"Dear God, help Dad find the pathway through the afterlife. Help him find his father and mother and find comfort in the relatives he had known as a young man and previously as a child. Also, I ask, that he be loved by the heavenly host of saints that went before and give him the peace he richly deserves."

FAILING MEMORY

All Dad's immediate family came to Dad's adult care home and the caregivers filtered in as well as the owner. I announced that Dad had passed to a better world. The men from the funeral home came in to remove him from his bed and take him to the mortuary. I said my last goodbye's to his physical body as they wheeled him out the door.

It did not stop me from thinking about him and remembering the good times I had as a child, the golf we played in Bend or the times he played with all his children and grandchildren before he passed. *Dad left a nice legacy.* I wish he could see all of his great grandchildren today. Now, I only have memories that I will share about him.

MEMORIES AND FORGETFULNESS

EPILOGUE – THE FUNERAL AND LEGACY

My mother, siblings and I knew Dad had shared a full life with so many people. In the end, however, his life diminished to caregivers waking him in the morning, changing him like a small child, being placed in a sling so that he could be transferred to his wheelchair with someone dressing him, brushing his teeth and hair. This was on top of him having to be wheeled to the TV for morning entertainment as he waited for breakfast and was fed his meal from a spoon and then he set in front of the TV until someone came to entertain him from the family. Then, the routine of being changed every two hours, fed lunch, more TV or whatever entertainment caregivers could provide as they cleaned the house. Then, caregivers would feed him dinner and conduct a routine that prepared him for bed. Ultimately, he did not talk, did not sing, and became totally reliant on the caregivers for his every need. His life did not have much meaning as we know it. But, from time to time I saw in his eyes and demeanor glimpses of the man I admired and loved.

MEMORIES AND FORGETFULNESS

Now, the relief and release occurred. Dad's relief gave way to my grief.

I spent the next few days talking to people at the funeral home making arrangements and helping Mother sign papers for Dad's final resting place. Then, I headed back home to meet my obligations at work in Oregon. Mother, my siblings and I planned a memorial service that was to be held at the Presbyterian Church where my parents worshiped on Valentine's Day, Saturday, February 14, 2009 2:00 p.m. It seemed to be the appropriate day for obvious reasons. We sent obituary announcements to the newspapers, friends and relatives telling them of Dad's passing.

To relieve my grief, I poured the next week into making memorial arrangements. I put together a slide show of Dad's life, showing joyful times and celebrations. I thought about how to stage his memorial; contemplating how to display the poignant and sublime memories I wanted to share. Therefore, I wrote a little speech to go along with the slide show. I wanted my siblings to each participate as well. I thought, the minister of the church certainly should have an appropriate sermon. I cleared all this with Mother and my siblings.

Valentine's Day came in a hurry and Carrie and I headed back to Lake Forest Park. On Friday evening, before the service, Mother offered her suggestions. My siblings and I prepared the setting for the memorial by practicing and preparing for the final curtain.

The gathering included my Dad's sister, Sarah and her family. Aunt Eva, my mother's sister, and her family were there. Also, church members, friends and family of my parents as well as my siblings attended the service. The sanctuary was full.

The service began by Mike and my Aunt Eva singing a haunting rendition of an old hymn. I first heard that song being sung a couple of years prior to this day by Dad and the daytime caregiver. He was still singing and humming tunes at that time. The caregiver would sing the first stanza and Dad would sing the second. One day, I walked in on them as they were singing together and they sounded great. I wanted to recreate that scene. I thought a rendition of the song may provide a glimpse into Dad's later stages of life at the adult care home.

MEMORIES AND FORGETFULNESS

After everyone came into the sanctuary and was seated, there was complete silence.

When Aunt Eva stood in the front of the congregation, she began to sing the first verse a cappella.

Then, from the back of the sanctuary, Mike began to sing the next verse.

And, Aunt Eva would counter with another verse.

Finally, Mike sung the last verse,

When they finished singing the song, Mike gave a little explanation about how Dad and his caregiver performed the hymn in the same manner with the interaction between them. This was meaningful as the words and music still rang in the ears of the congregants.

The large gathering of people listened attentively to the family as we talked about Dad and sang our way through the rest of the memorial service. The media person in the balcony showed my slide presentation of Dad's life. The pastor gave a moving account of my parent's involvement in the church. She spoke about Dad helping around the church and how kind he was to everyone.

EPILOGUE

Each one of my siblings and I gave a remembrance of my father.

Many people came to the funeral that I had not seen since childhood and when they were re-introduced to me, we had a good laugh about the early days. More importantly, I had a feeling of appreciation because so many remembered Dad affectionately.

I can say that most everyone who attended the service told stories about my father and how he touched their lives. I expressed my gratitude to them because their memories of "my Dad" reconnected me to him, relatives, friends and our community.

I knew he lived a life well executed and remembered.

A few weeks later, we placed Dad's ashes in the cemetery in Bothell, Washington. This was a much smaller gathering, of family and friends who attended the service. They told additional stories of Dad and once again confirmed that his life was well lived.

I look back on Dad's life and I cannot imagine God not being pleased with how he lived. For me, Dad's love and enjoyment of life, family as well as friends remain strong in my mind. I have lasting memories of Dad's stories about his experiences that inspires me with every step and footfall I take. I am surrounded by Dad's family, friends and acquaintances who knew the joy he spread to the world.

As mother said, "He was here to love and be loved." It is a warm and memorable farewell.

My faith and belief tell me I may one day reunite with my Dad.

ABOUT THE AUTHOR:

Larry Calkins was raised in the state of Washington. He attended a University located in Washington State. After graduation, he worked in Oregon as an Environmental Specialist. When he retired from being a state employee, Larry and his wife moved to Arizona where they currently reside.

Since retiring, Larry became interested in his family history, longed to understand his family's roots and to understand family members as individuals. This desire prompted him to write a book like this one. Other books written or published by Larry Calkins include:

To Endure – Rekindled Love; Stories of Travis Calkins
> By Larry Calkins

The Journal of Catherine Howland Bourne
> By Emma Taber Bourne

Loring Gary Calkins Senior Art Work
> A pictorial essay

MEMORIES AND FORGETFULNESS

Made in the USA
Monee, IL
09 February 2023